Paws And Purpose

Inspiring Animal Tales of Healing and Transformation

Compiled By Kyra Schaefer

Paws And Purpose: Inspiring Animal Tales of Healing and Transformation

Copyright © 2024 by As You Wish Publishing

All rights reserved.

ISBN: 978-1-951131-67-8

No portion of this book may be reproduced in any form without written permission from the publisher, As You Wish Publishing connect@asyouwishpublishing.com, except as permitted by U.S. copyright law.

Not a substitute for mental, emotional or physical medical advice. All author's opinions are their own. If you need help please seek out a medical professional for advice.

Contents

1. Avery, Animal Protector — 1
   By Natacha Belair

2. Whatever Lola Wants — 9
   By Stacy Christopher

3. Unleashing Love: A Journey of Hope, Healing, and Connections — 17
   By Danielle Darowz

4. Divine Pawpose: How Stars and Angels Led to Peace and Quiet — 27
   By Beth Eiglarsh

5. An Animal Communicator's Awakening — 35
   By Keri Glaser

6. All The Water Was Falling From The Sky — 43
   By Karen Gabler

7. Returning the Favor — 51
   By Sarah Gabler

8. Monkey: The Dog Who Changed My Life — 57
   By Dr. Sushma D.A. Hallock

9. Faith Creates Miracles — 65
   By Erica Hess

10.	Bridge of Discovery: My Parkway Journey By Marnie Hollander	73
11.	From Heartbreak to Hoofbeats By Amy I King	81
12.	Princess's Odyssey: A Tale of Love Healing Pain By Dr. Sally Nazari	89
13.	Ruby Returns By Rosanne Groover Norris	105
14.	27 Dogs By Natasha Pecarski	113
15.	Fluffy Furry Fairy By Sylvie Robert	121
16.	Essence Over Form By Kyra Schaefer	133
17.	Lessons From An Enchanted Peanut By YuSon Shin	139
18.	By the Grace of a Dog By Alicia Sweezer	151
19.	Animal Teachers By Kristen West	159
20.	Whispers of Wisdom: A Journey through Animal Insights and Personal Discoveries By Hellevi Woodman	165
21.	The Journey Home, Healing, and Self-Love By Janet Zavala	181

Animal Gallery	187
Featured Authors	201

Chapter One
Avery, Animal Protector
By Natacha Belair

I dedicate this short story to my fur and scale babies—past and present. Thank you for your everlasting companionship, love, and affection, and for teaching me so much about myself.

My name's Avery Westwater, and I'm fifteen years old. I'm Natacha Belair's alter ego. She brought me to life several years ago to share her out-of-body adventure with the world.

I used to be a regular teen—focused on school, soccer, friends, and boys. That all changed when I experienced my first-ever lucid dream where I traveled to another dimension that looked like our galaxy—endless black space speckled with millions of stars and distant planets. This is when I discovered that I'm an animal protector and that I'm but one of ten thousand individuals who were recently evoked to their true purpose—to help save

Earth from human destruction before it's too late.

But was it only a dream?

During my interdimensional visits, I uncovered many of my past lives and realized that I'm always surrounded by critters. For example, in the life I held before this one, my soulmate and I found ourselves in the right place at the right time and adopted countless creatures in need. Was it happenstance or kismet? I invite you to keep reading and decide for yourself.

Approximately one year after our second child was born, my father spent a few days at his friend's farm. This was when a shorthair black-brown Mackerel Tabby kitten with the cutest cream-colored nose and mesmerizing hazelnut eyes with beige highlights befriended my dad. She even jumped into his car when he was packing his belongings to head back home.

My husband and I hadn't had a pet in quite some time, which was odd for us but perfect as we spent most of our energy raising two small children. However, my highly intuitive father knew we were ready to welcome a new fur baby into our household, and he was right. He offered to take care of everything. A few weeks went by, and he introduced me to one of my soul sisters. Lexie and I instantly bonded and shared an inexplicable connection that filled my heart and spirit with unconditional love.

A decade later, my husband stumbled upon Shelby—an endearing black puppy with random white spots on her toes, muzzle and scruff—who longed for her forever family. An elderly man we knew had purchased a Boston Terrier a few months after his wife had suddenly passed. He was looking forward to having another soul in his now empty house, but he quickly realized he couldn't care for such an energetic being.

This sweet and spirited six-month-old pup brought a lot of activity into our home, and I loved it. Lexie, on the other hand, who was eleven years old at the time, wasn't a fan at first. She eventually got used to her new sister's random bouts of hyperactivity, they both learned to respect each other's boundaries, and they became close friends—often spending long afternoons cuddled on the couch.

Approximately four years later, Shelby noticed an animal whimpering outside on a cold and windy early spring evening. She whined and barked until she gained my husband's attention. We promptly added layers and headed to the alleyway in front of our house. This was when we discovered a large white dog tied to a fence—abandoned. Our hearts instantly melted for this defenseless animal who featured sympathetic mint eyes and rose-colored nose and ears.

This gentle soul spent over three weeks at the Humane Society, where the veterinary staff assessed his health and behavior. They provided a full medical workup, which included vaccinations, neutering, and a deep dental cleaning where they had to remove four rotten teeth.

We anxiously waited for the shelter to call, and the whole family was relieved when we received the green light to adopt this one-and-a-half-year-old Dogo Argentino/Pitt Bull mix we named Jax. Although Shelby and Jax were different in weight, size, and color, they quickly became best friends and could've passed as siblings with their short hair, large ears, and muscular bodies. This became especially true when Jax started to emulate his big sister and act like a hyperactive mammoth-sized Boston Terrier.

When we shared Jax's origin story with our friends and loved ones, most expressed feelings of anger and disgust at his past owners. My response was always the same, "Jax is part of our soul family, and the universe brought him to us. His past owners picked the right alley to make it happen, and I'm grateful."

Many moons later—after having mourned the loss of our beloved Lexie, Shelby, and Jax—I heard slight scratching sounds coming from one of our basement windows. I opened the blinds to discover a Turkish Angora kitten who'd made her way through the mounds of snow piled around the house. I quickly put on my winter jacket and boots and headed outside. She almost ran away when she saw me approach but eventually crouched and looked directly into my soul with her piercing blue eyes. This is when I knew this helpless being conceded to the circumstances and gave me permission to scoop her up gently.

She smelled like fuel, her fur was covered in black gunk, and seven of her toes were frostbitten. My husband and I bathed her and dried her beautiful white fluffy coat with my hairdryer set on low. She closed her eyes and relished in the toasty breeze. The next morning, we brought her to the veterinarian, who assumed this three-month-old kitten had spent at least a few days hiding under car hoods to keep warm. He also said that her frostbitten toes indicated that she would've frozen to death if she hadn't found refuge when she did.

We immediately brought this gorgeous creature home and named her Bella. She seamlessly infused herself into our lives and hearts as though she'd always been part of our soul family. Truth be told, I often saw a glimpse of Jax when I looked into Bella's adoring eyes.

From my experience, I can state that sheltered or abandoned animals make the best companions—they understand what you did for them, they're forever grateful, and they'll show their appreciation for you every day. My fur and scale rescue babies filled my soul with love, taught me lessons I didn't even know I had to learn, and made me a better human.

I hope these few words will inspire you to join me in my quest to slow and eventually stop the pet manufacturing industry. Meanwhile, please remember—you don't have to be an awoken animal protector to relate to all living things and empathize with them—open your heart and follow your instincts. Next time you stumble upon a distressed critter, ground yourself to your higher power; direct a portion of the positive universal energy you're attracting to the creature in front of you, and your natural ability to share your love with those in need will take over.

I hope you liked learning about me (Natacha), my alter ego (Avery) and our innate connection to animals and our quest to help heal our beautiful planet so it may thrive for millennia. Although I couldn't resist including some fantastical flair, please know that I wrote these few pages based on facts.

If you enjoyed reading this short story, I have a feeling

you'd appreciate my young adult fiction novels. My goal when writing is to create intriguing and enigmatic stories that introduce tweens and teens to mind/body/spirit concepts—such as living one's true purpose, karmic energy, past lives, and interstellar travel—and hopefully, encourage this generation to come up with innovative ways to fix the mistakes of those who lived on Earth before them.

Bio

Natacha Belair is the Award-Winning Author behind the *A Stellar Purpose* trilogy—a unique and thought-provoking narrative that uses fantasy to address real-life topics such as animal rights, environmental care, and positive social change. In these novels, Natacha masterfully intertwines memorable characters with colorful backdrops and mind-boggling theories—delivering captivating, sci-fi-filled adventures set in inspirational storylines.

When she's not writing or chatting with her fans, Natacha enjoys spending warm days outdoors with her husband, two teenage daughters, and her fur and scale babies.
To learn more, visit www.NatachaBelair.com.

Praise for *A Stellar Purpose*

"A beautiful narrative of what might be possible for

humanity."
—Jim Self, Mastering Alchemy

"A timely, unique, and creative story."
—Emily Keefer, Author

"A book intended for adolescents that adults will love too."
—Wally Jones, Multi-Award-Winning Author

"*A Stellar Purpose* is stellar indeed."
—Grace Jackson, Book Critic

Praise for *A Stellar Purpose II*

"Will make you ponder on your unique talents to help heal humanity and Earth herself."
—Linda J. Crane, Anthropogenic Global Warming and Environmental Activist

"A spellbinding and captivating journey."
—Bill Sheehan, Award-Winning Author

"Will appeal to animal and nature lovers."
—Myriam Thauvette, High School Librarian

"A truly inspiring novel."
—Mégane Bilodeau, Book Critic

Chapter Two
Whatever Lola Wants
By Stacy Christopher

Question: How can you tell if someone's vegan? Answer: Wait two minutes, they'll tell you.

Well, that didn't take the full two minutes, so please allow me to backtrack and share the story of how a little dog with a huge personality opened my eyes, mind and heart in a way that completely transformed my life. Twelve years ago, we were mourning the loss of a dear family friend I'll call "Angel," who left this world very unexpectedly and much too young. To honor the memory of this beautiful soul, I decided to volunteer at our local animal rescue. Angel had volunteered there, finding tremendous peace in comforting the strays.

After completing the volunteer training, I had my first official shift with my new team. One room we entered had three dogs listed on the whiteboard, but only two greeted us. A note explained that the third dog, Mindee, had been hiding behind the couch since her arrival; we were to just block off both ends and clean around her.

When I crouched down to get a glimpse of the little recluse, she darted out and launched herself at me, then clung to my neck, quivering. Mindee was nine months old, a white Chihuahua-Rat Terrier mix with brown spots. She had one brown eye and one blue eye. I knew that Angel had ethereally shooed her out from behind the couch and into my heart. I couldn't stop thinking about her. When I arrived at the shelter's next adoption event, I was told that she had growled and snapped at everyone who tried to approach her, with the comically outraged ferocity that only a small Chihuahua can display. When she saw me, she threw herself at me again. I didn't need another sign.

The rescue brought her over for a home safety check and meet-and-greet with our dog, Howie, who was from another shelter. Howie was a Chihuahua-Pug mix, so easy-going and charming that I thought of him as George Clooney in canine form. He regarded her affably, and before he could attempt to establish his seniority, she scuttled over and started humping his shin. Startled, he looked at her for a moment, then licked her face tenderly. It was a done deal. Mindee was home.

The name the county had given her when she came in as a stray didn't feel like a good fit, and my son suggested "Lola." He had performed in his high school's production of *Damn Yankees*, and the song "Whatever Lola Wants, Lola Gets" was still fresh in our minds. It suited her perfectly since she completely ignored being called by her government name. She responded to "Lola" immediately.

Within days, it was impossible to remember life before Lola. She cowered when another dog approached, only to spin around and bark furiously once they'd passed. Her anxiety issues gained her the nicknames "Baby Shakes" and "Tremble Rat," yet she guarded her dental chews with a snarling vengeance. She was a stealthy little hoarder, stashing treats, toys and socks into little piles for me to find while cleaning. Soon, there were songs that revolved around her, including (with apologies to The Kinks): "Lola, she's bubbly like cola, too shy to say hola," and "Her name was Lola, her eyes were crazy," sung to the tune of Barry Manilow's "Copacabana." On cold days, she refused to move if I put a coat on her, glaring at me intensely as if she might burst into flames. I realized that, deep down, Lola and I were the same person.

About six months after Angel sent Lola our way, I left her and Howie in charge and went to see a friend play Bob Cratchit in *A Christmas Carol*. When I got home, the smoke detector was beeping at top volume because the battery was low. Howie barked at me with some irritation as I fumbled to replace it. But when I called Lola, she didn't come running. I assumed she was hiding from the noise, but I couldn't find her anywhere. I checked our little patio, thinking she might have gone out through the doggy door to escape the racket. With a horrible sinking feeling, I realized that if she'd stayed out there for any length of time, she'd have been fair game for hawks, owls, coyotes or any other local wildlife.

I grabbed a flashlight and ran outside, then beat the bushes and traipsed through the underbrush for hours, calling her name. The longer I searched, the worse the images in my mind became. I pictured her wounded, bleeding, terrified, "dead in a ditch," the expression that parents use when their kids haven't called. I finally made my way home and crawled into bed, filthy and sobbing. There was a movement, and I reached out for Howie, knowing he would be as devastated as I was by our loss. But it wasn't Howie who started licking my face. It was Lola. She had managed to find a tiny hiding space under the bed, between a storage container and the wall, where I hadn't seen her any of the times I'd looked. As the most incredible relief flooded over me, she yapped shrilly in my face, annoyed that I'd been gone so long.

This is where we circle back to the beginning of my story. The next morning, I recoiled at the sight of virtually everything in my refrigerator. All the meat, eggs, and dairy products turned my stomach because I immediately associated them with the graphic mental images of fear and suffering from the night before. That was it. I became a vegan at that precise moment. I emptied the fridge and cabinets, donated and passed along as much as I could and discarded the rest. Out went the leather, silk and wool from my closet. Out went anything that was tested on animals, including my cigarettes. Mark Twain wisely observed that "Giving up smoking is the easiest thing in the world. I know because I've done it thousands of times." I had, too, in my decades-long love affair with cigarettes, but this time it stuck.

In my twenties, I'd read somewhere that if everyone would stop eating meat for two years, world hunger would end, so I did. Two years later, I went cheerfully back to burgers, feeling that I'd done my part. But it wasn't an abstract concept anymore, not after that horrible night. It was so intensely personal that the change was effortless. Once the connection happened in my mind, I couldn't un-see it. For someone who overthinks everything to the point of absolute exhaustion, it was nothing short of a miracle.

As funny as I find the joke I opened with, I don't talk about my vegan lifestyle unless someone asks. I'm happy to let people think whatever they like (although the part where I stopped smoking always goes over well). I agree wholeheartedly with Alice Walker that "Advocacy is the rent I pay for living on the planet," but I couldn't have imagined the revelations it would bring. My advocacy for animals is a journey that has profoundly deepened my spiritual beliefs and practices. I still volunteer at the same shelter, and every day, I become more keenly aware of how much animals can teach us about trust, unconditional love and loyalty, and living in the present moment. I owe it all to a sweet, stubborn, spunky, crazy-eyed bundle of sass named Lola, and the absolute Angel who brought us together.

Lola and Howie are across the Rainbow Bridge now, with their fur-brother Monkey, who joined our family later. (You can read about Monkey in this book's chapter, which was written by his auntie, Dr. Sushma Hallock.) The day I sat down to write this, Howie and Monkey sent me enthusiastic signs of happiness that their sister's story was being shared (a condensation trail in a bright blue sky and a squirrel who paused mid-scamper to make prolonged eye contact, respectively). Now, as I finish, my neighbor's smoke alarm is suddenly blasting at top volume, so I know that Lola approves. Always and forever, baby girl—whatever you want.

Bio

Stacy Christopher (she/her) is an ordained minister, Reiki Master and licensed therapist. It has been her absolute honor to study with the Rev. Dr. Michael Beckwith, globally beloved psychic medium Tony Stockwell, "Psychic Sergeant" Peter Close, renowned animal communicator Elizabeth Ayer Lee, and award-winning podcast creator Ann Theato. Stacy loves working with open-minded creatives on their journey to increase motivation and direction via aligning with their inner guidance. Her passions include advocating for justice and equality, volunteering in animal rescue and being a huge theater nerd.

Website: TheBloomingMystic.com
FB/IG: The Blooming Mystic

Chapter Three
Unleashing Love: A Journey of Hope, Healing, and Connections
By Danielle Darowz

As the French novelist Anatole France once stated, "Until one has loved an animal, a part of one's soul remains unawakened." As I reflect on my journey, I recall that pivotal moment when I agreed to foster and how it felt. Unknowingly, that decision would lead to a soulful connection with the dogs in my care. A bond that transcends mere companionship.

All fosters are unique personalities, and we all start somewhere. When looking into their eyes, my heart felt a remarkable warmth. I could see their furry bodies relax and feel the relief of being safe. They may be here for part of our lives, but we are all they have. It is our responsibility to love, nurture, and protect. Amidst the joyful moments, challenges arise, revealing your resilience when confronted with life-and-death decisions. You discover unexpected strength in overcoming obstacles.

Accompanied by my first foster and soul dog, Rocky, I embarked on fostering again. I had taken a hiatus to mend my heart following the loss of my first dog. Occasionally, the universe sends you the help and healing you need in different forms. Looking back from then to now, there were countless moments of heartache, career shifts, work travels, and the blossoming of a new marriage. It's a tale brimming with emotions, but for now, let's return to that pivotal moment—the next foster, "Yes!"—and focus on the delightful puppy that changed so many hearts and a community.

When the opportunity arose for me to foster once more, it was to care for two puppies. As we drove to pick up the new fosters, my stomach churned with anticipation. These little lives had traveled from Kentucky to Buffalo, guided by a dedicated volunteer. Left in a box outside a shelter, they carried stories of resilience. Now, I stood in a parking lot, cradling a brown puppy and a black puppy, unaware of how profoundly one of them would change my world. No matter what a dog has been through before they come into your life, they still find a way to trust and love you. A lesson we can all learn from.

I had never raised a puppy before. My previous dogs had always been fully grown. Honestly, they were always big lap dogs that thought they were the size of a puppy. What awaited me now? I took a deep breath and braced myself. And so began a new chapter—a journey of strength, hope, and the transformative power of saying yes.

Thankfully, our dogs quickly bonded with the newcomers. Rocky, the older sibling, eagerly played, and Sadie, a former momma dog we rescued, showed her maternal instincts with such sass better than any human could. However, within about a week, things took a dramatic turn.

As we returned home from our weekly Sunday dinner at my parents' place, our black puppy named Pia suddenly began emitting a high-pitched sound I had never heard before. She appeared unsteady and was pressing her head against the wall. When I picked her up, she gazed at me with a blank stare before falling unconscious in my arms. Feeling helpless, I quickly called the rescue and the emergency clinic. When fostering, you are at the mercy of the rescue, which has limited funds. Despite financial constraints, they are rich in compassion. I rushed out of the house with Pia in my arms, secured her in the car, and I was on my way. Throughout the drive to the clinic, I stayed focused and made sure she was still breathing. But I don't think I breathed the entire ride.

After an evening of evaluations, it was discovered that

Pia had a rare portosystemic liver shunt, an abnormal condition causing toxins to poison her system. Medically treating this condition leaves only one-third of dogs with a long life, and she was at risk for seizures and liver damage. Navigating calls with the rescue, every decision became critical. Fortunately, a compassionate decision was made to give Pia a chance.

The next day, news spread about a critically ill foster in need of life-saving surgery, prompting an unprecedented community rally. With the green light given, Pia was stabilized for the intricate liver shunt surgery performed by a skilled surgeon. With continual updates on Pia's progress, local donations and donations as far away as Hawaii poured in. Looking back, it was surreal.

Pia made it through the surgery, and now thousands of people were invested in her story and collectively focused on her healing. During the surgery, it was discovered that all her organs, including her heart, were on the opposite side. It's a true rarity. From day one, Pia displayed unwavering determination and a strong will to live. Then, the unthinkable happened. She developed sepsis. I received a call at work detailing a peritonitis complication, a life-threatening situation requiring another immediate surgery. I'll never forget that phone call; trying to keep it together at work, I could feel my body begin to tremble. The hospital, acknowledging she was a rescue, questioned the financial commitment, forcing both me and the rescue into a corner. Despite the overwhelming anxiety, community support prevailed, and the second green light was given. Against all odds, Pia triumphed.

We initiated a blog to provide regular updates on Pia. The posts became a daily morning ritual for many invested in her remarkable story. Pia became quite the local celebrity, even inspiring a feature by the news, affectionately dubbing her the Easter Miracle Puppy.

Regardless of differences, animals have a unique ability to unite people. Upon her return to my care, we rallied together. Juggling with work hours, we devised a plan for her recovery. A team of volunteers helped each afternoon with her special feeding and medication schedule. A true testament to the saying, "It takes a village."

As with all fosters, you know that eventually, they will need a "fur-ever" home. Many people thought I was going to keep her after nurturing her for many months. I knew intuitively, though, that her perfect home existed. Fostering her was a unique commitment that mended my heart and forged connections with the rescue, the community, and friends, leading to new friendships.

When it was time to find Pia's forever home, we faced an overwhelming number of applications. Fortunately, in the most synchronistic way, the perfect home was recommended by a favorite vet while I was at the animal hospital for one of my dogs. Pia's new mom, unaware of Pia's local celebrity status, had recently lost her dog and was recovering from cancer. Their connection felt right, and Pia's role became more profound as she brought healing to her new mom.

Pia thrived in a beautiful home, spending summers at the Jersey Shore, attending church, and delivering meals to the elderly. This rags-to-riches tale, in addition to a friendship with her new mom, led to delightful dinner memories and a lasting habit of ordering "proper dinners." I'll never forget when I ordered an open-faced turkey sandwich, she said, "Danielle, you should order a proper dinner with a knife and fork." I still giggle about this, and to this day, I order a proper dinner.

Soon after Pia was adopted, we hosted a celebration barbeque at our home to thank every person who was part of her journey. Many were people who came to our home during the workday (many on their lunch breaks) and cared for her. It was a beautiful outdoor afternoon with the sun shining over us, laughter filling the yard, and sharing our stories. We were grateful that Pia's new mom, accompanied by Pia and her granddaughter, were able to meet her angels.

Years later, I received a call that Pia's mom unexpectedly passed away. Pia stayed by her side for days. A true testament to a faithful companion. When the authorities gave Pia to a family friend, I came back to town, picked her up, and brought her to my home again. Eventually, Pia settled into her new home with her mom's daughter and lived a beautiful life with her human and fur sister, helping them heal from their loss.

This journey, initiated by a simple "yes," illustrates the transformative power of animals. Pia healed many hearts in her lifetime. Every animal that has come into my life has become a permanent part of my heart, gifting a legacy of love, healing, and friendship.

Bio

Danielle Darowz is a Certified Spiritual Advisor, psychic medium, and animal intuitive with a heart-driven journey, having completed advanced studies in telepathic communication with animals. For over two decades, she's been a guiding force in animal rescue, co-founding nonprofits to champion their cause alongside a successful 20-year career in information technology. She utilizes her spiritual gifts to provide healing and guidance to both humans and their beloved pets. Danielle stands as a beacon of compassion, skillfully uniting the spiritual realms to connect souls and cultivate a balance between the earthly and metaphysical dimensions. For more, visit www.danielledarowz.com or follow on Instagram @danielledarowz

"Each soul enters the earthly realm with the intent to enrich not only their experience but also others. These soul mates embark on a shared journey with the mutual goal of growth and development. Much like we choose our parents to aid in mastering specific life lessons, our pets choose us when our need for them is greatest. The magnitude of the union isn't fully realized until they've passed."

Beth Eiglarsh

Chapter Four
Divine Pawpose: How Stars and Angels Led to Peace and Quiet
By Beth Eiglarsh

It was the pinnacle of a clean-slate Monday—it was January 1st—a day I had long anticipated for what felt like forever. A chance to transition into a year markedly different from the previous one, dominated by health challenges and dis-ease. An opportunity to make a U-turn back to a life filled with upward momentum and contentment. I woke up with palpable positivity, driven by my inside voice that believed "whatever transpires today will set the tone for the rest of the year." A whimsical notion, I admit. I would go to my happy place, the magical park nearby, and incorporate cardio, commune with nature, and have a chat with God. I would meditate, soak up the wisdom of the 150-year-old oaks, and bottle this invincible energy for the remaining 364 days. Then my 1-year-old goldendoodle glanced at me with her irresistible eyes.

She threw up on the console before we exited my development. I used a t-shirt to clean the mess, but not before she stepped in it. I needed a bigger t-shirt. The minute her paws touched the ground, she pooped. Uh-oh, where are my doggie bags? Filled with awe and wonder that likened to a career criminal released from jail for the first time, she chased every squirrel, terrorized every duck, and fully committed to smelling every blade of grass. Without warning, she dashed toward another dog and pulled me to the floor. As the embarrassment of having an unruly child washed over me, I knew I had a choice. I regained my composure and began to look for the message in the mess.

Soul Mission

Each soul enters the earthly realm with the intent to enrich not only their experience but also others. These soul mates embark on a shared journey with the mutual goal of growth and development. Much like we choose our parents to aid in mastering specific life lessons, our pets choose us when our need for them is greatest. The magnitude of the union isn't fully realized until they've passed.

Similar to humans, dogs possess unique callings that guide them in their roles. Whether to hunt, protect, pull a sled in the Olympics, or provide emotional support, a dog's innate purpose is to be there, to be present.

> *"People are born so they can learn how to live a good life. Like loving everybody all the time, and being nice. Well, dogs already know how to do that so they don't have to stay that long."*
> *~ anonymous 6 yr old*

With my steadfast mission to cement a good year, I shifted my focus at the park. I decided that instead of getting frustrated with my dog, I would learn from her. She approached every person without judgment, completely unattached to the outcome. She explored unfamiliar places with unyielding enthusiasm. She stopped at all the water fountains, teaching me the importance of honoring her needs. With her playful and curious spirit, she reminded me that life is inherently uncomplicated and that even the smallest things are worthy of excitement.

I was grateful for my furry companion and reflected on all those that came into my life before her. I had been surrounded by unconditional love, at all the right moments, and was granted the gift of paws.

Meet Starr

"I'm so sorry," said Dr Cesar Rosa, the specialist who delivered the devastating news. The ultrasound not only revealed the sex of our baby, a surprise we had hoped to save for labor day, but also showed the brain protruding from the skull that hadn't closed properly. It was a boy.

After delivering our son at 20 weeks, we returned home to an eerily empty house. The nursery was prepared, Goodnight Moon was on the rocking chair, and a copy of *What To Expect When You Are Expecting* lay on the kitchen counter. *We didn't expect this.*

To lift our spirits, my husband surprised me with a yellow lab puppy. We named her Starr. Following the doctor's orders, we quadrupled our folic acid and tried again. Like clockwork, we were pregnant. Two weeks before our son was born, Starr tragically passed after ingesting a softball that became entangled in her intestines and sent her into toxic shock. The scream that poured out of my husband mirrored my internal anguish when hearing the heartbreaking news that our first son wouldn't survive outside the womb.

Starr's purpose was brief, yet powerful—to give us an outlet for the pent-up love we had reserved for our baby. Thank you, Starr, for being our angel.

Meet Angel

I hit rock bottom. I was an anxiety-ridden workaholic, without a spiritual tool to my name. My back pain morphed into emotional pain. My life was a chaotic mess, my marriage was strained and I dropped all of the balls I was juggling. Seeking help, I left home for 2 months.

During my time of self-reflection, I found a true gift in awareness that radically shifted my perspective and prepared me for a life that aligned with my true mission. But what about the learning curve? As I prepared to return home to my husband and 3, 5, and 7-year-old, I questioned their idea of getting a new puppy. With little time to contemplate, here came our first goldendoodle.

Through training and adjustment, Angel transformed into an angel—my angel. She shadowed me, comforted me, loved me, and supported me. Every visitor in our home fell in love and agreed that she was a human disguised as a dog. Angel became my emotional anchor and Robin to my Batman, through my spiritual transformation.

As Angel aged, we decided to introduce another puppy to keep her youthful spirit alive. Managing two dogs was challenging, but we caught glimpses of a growing bond. The new doodle was obsessed with her big sister. Unfortunately, Angel developed a cough and three months later passed away in my arms after a heart tumor was discovered.

Angel's purpose was golden. She taught me resilience

during a pivotal time in my life. Our connection remained unbreakable. Thank you, Angel, for bringing me peace.

Meet Peace

Peace was confused when Angel didn't come home. As she pondered the new household dynamics, we questioned if the correct dog had been delivered. She was cream-colored. We wanted white. Snow white, exactly like Angel. We called and asked if we received "pink collar girl" or if they inadvertently swapped the dogs. My 16-year-old son screamed in the background, "You guys are crazy! She's a dog and she's adorable and I want to keep her." My 18-year-old daughter chimed in, "Let me know if I can start loving her now." We realized how ridiculous we were acting. Deep down, I sensed that Peace had chosen us and that there were no mistakes. She brought an unexpected gift with her—a lesson in flexibility.

Peace has become the love of our lives, with each family member treasuring their unique relationship. Day by day, she embodies her name more fully, offering peace-full moments and unwavering loyalty.

Peace's purpose was to ease the pain of losing Angel. It was also to provide a source of tender affection as I leaped through uncomfortable hurdles. When my mind was racing with loud thoughts, Peace reminded me that I could embrace tranquility, even amid uncertainty. Thank you, Peace, for the quiet.

Meet Quiet

My 17-year-old son is a high school senior. This fall, he will head off to college, and we will welcome our newest family member, a snow-white mini doodle. With three kids out of the house, we will become empty nesters. We will finally have Peace and Quiet.

Her purpose speaks for itself.

Bio

Beth is an NLP Life Coach, AP Reiki Master, HMR Trauma Healer, Spiritual Teacher, and Empathic Intuitive. She is a perpetual student, who values the wisdom she acquired through her diverse experiences. Her gift lies in empowering others to embrace their stories, using *her* story as the foundation for her teachings.

Before her spiritual awakening, Beth struggled with chaos, chronic pain, and workaholism. She underwent an intense introspective process and made a radical pivot, creating a system for living to help others navigate their lives with greater ease and grace. She teaches groups and individuals how to raise their level of *Awareness*,

Remember who they are, *Manifest* their desires, and be of *Service* to themselves and others, using her A.R.M.S. formula.

An "International Best-Selling Author," Beth penned *Beth's Case Scenario: Journey from Chaos to Emotional Freedom,* now available in audiobook format. This is her 5th collaborative book with As You Wish Publishing, and she is immeasurably grateful for the connections made. She seizes every opportunity to help people feel better by offering one-on-one sessions, workshops, and Mind, Body, and Spirit retreats. For more information, go to www.SpeakToBeth.com

Chapter Five

An Animal Communicator's Awakening

By Keri Glaser

Yes, you read that right. It reads Psychic Medium *and* Animal Communicator. Not only does that mean I can talk to spirits, but I also talk to animals. Seems crazy, right? In some cases, that may be so, but I love the work I do. I'm grateful every day for my clients and the opportunities I have to connect with them.

However, animal communication was not a ride I thought I would be taking. I had worked with people who communicated with animals before and thought it was *fascinating*, but it wasn't in my wheelhouse. I mean, talking to human spirits was enough for me at times. Occasionally, I would receive small messages from animals for their humans, but it wasn't anything to get excited about.

Experienced intuitives say that while hanging around others in our community, their abilities and gifts often rub off or help us give rise to those abilities. I do love animals and have always felt a connection with them on a higher level. It wasn't until I experienced personal situations with my animals, Maggie and Willow, that I felt owning the ability to be an animal communicator was something I should be doing. I am blessed to have many animal communication stories since opening up with Maggie and Willow and letting myself trust more in my communication.

My most recent experience is helping friends cross their fur loves over. I was able to hear them. I'm not sure how, but I just know what to say and tell the family along the way. I always hope that it brings comfort and even closure. I have been told it does, so I trust in their response.

I also talk to living animals and help communicate between them and their humans. That still blows my mind sometimes because it's usually about behavior, how and why they behave the way they do. Animals are very truthful. So truthful, in fact, that their humans often find out that what they are acting out about is something the human is doing or not doing.

The first time I truly experienced hearing or knowing what an animal needed was with my dog, Maggie. As she was passing on, I could feel what she needed, almost as if it were what she was telling me. I knew she was ready to leave this living place and go home to be with my dad. I immediately told our Veterinarian that she didn't want a test; she was ready to go, and we wanted to make sure she was comfortable. After a while I could physically feel she was having trouble letting go, so I asked her if she wanted help. I heard, "Yes." She was ready to rest. My husband was nervous and talking for what seemed like a mile a minute. I heard Maggie say, "Tell him I'm okay, and I love him too." After settling him, I was able to hold Mag as she crossed. I watched my sweet girl go through a gate right up to my dad. I knew she was happy and healthy again, running and playing. She even let me know her cat brother was there waiting to play. I can't tell you how or what I was experiencing at that time, but I wasn't on this earth while she passed. I was in another mind space.

A month or so later, we began to feel the emptiness of not having Maggie around anymore. We started looking at rescue sites for dogs that needed homes. We had found a few we thought would be great in our home. We have a cat so it was important they got along with cats. It seemed like every dog we liked, or thought was the one, was either adopted or pending adoption. So we stopped looking, thinking it just wasn't time for a new energy, but one day, my brother-in-law called. He asked my husband if we found a dog yet. He knew of one needing a home that was being fostered, so he sent a picture. Naturally, I fell in *love* and just *had* to meet her.

She had been through a lot in her short lifetime. Her poor little botched ears looked like someone used dull scissors instead of the correct bobbing method. Her talk was nonexistent. She didn't like her back area being touched for the longest time. Her legs had healed by the time she got to our home, but they had been broken at one time. From what we heard, she healed herself. This poor girl was a mess with issues we didn't know or see at the time. She had begun lunging at us and then biting. Her name was originally Zippy because after her legs healed, she zipped around like crazy with the zoomies. We liked the name, but she didn't seem to respond well to it. She never came when called, and her hearing was proven fine. We tried a few names, but she was having issues. It got to a point where we thought it might be better to find her a home that could handle this beautiful mess. I was especially having a hard time with this. My dad taught us we never give up on people or dogs just because they experience challenges.

As I was waking up one morning talking aloud to spirit (as I often do at this time), I asked for help with her. Did she belong with us? I heard very clearly, "My name is Willow." No one was home with us. It was just me, our cat, and the dog. I sat for a minute thinking, what the heck? I stood out of bed and walked down the hall to the other room. Willow's door to her "house" was open. She was like a brand-new dog. To this day, we still have a unique connection.

The next year with Willow was a lot of touch and go, and I learned a new language of communication with her that I hadn't had with previous dogs. This led me to open up more, talking with more animals, trusting that I could hear and feel what they needed to communicate.

Bio

Keri is internationally known for her Psychic Medium/Animal Communication connections with years of experience. She enjoys the opportunity to sit with clients in person, on the phone or by Facetime, making their time together more personal. Whether human or animal, Keri treats every client like she's known them for a lifetime. She embodies empathy and compassion for all, thriving on providing the best in every sitting. Keri's readings are full of information and profound insight. If you have not seen Keri in a gallery or party setting, you are missing out! Her galleries are amazing to watch as she is known to engage the entire audience. Even if you don't receive a personal reading, you will leave the gallery with a message. For over two decades of professional psychic work, Keri presents an extensive repeat clientele with high-praise results. Though spirit communication is never a guarantee, she will answer your question to the best of her abilities by bridging the spirit realm with her connection. Clients typically report her readings as exactly what they need and the sense of peace provided after.

www.keriglaser-psychic-medium.com
keriglaser@gmail.com

"If we spent more time connecting with our animals, we would learn how to embrace our blessings, let go of our challenges, and enhance our life experiences."

Karen Gabler

Chapter Six
All The Water Was Falling From The Sky
By Karen Gabler

When I began using my intuitive gifts to communicate with animals, I wasn't surprised to hear some of the things they wanted to convey: I like my new food, my last treats were yummier, I'd rather sleep than work, and similar day-to-day surface concerns we would assume animals would focus upon. What surprised me is how deeply they understand what really matters, how quickly they embrace their purpose in our lives, and how easily they share important life lessons with us. If we spent more time connecting with our animals, we would learn how to embrace our blessings, let go of our challenges, and enhance our life experiences.

As a long-time horse owner and rider, I've been lucky to have a steady supply of horses at my barn to connect with. It is inspiring and thought-provoking to experience the world through their eyes and consider the lessons they've shared with me along the way.

Look at the World from a New Perspective

California was drenched in torrential rains for weeks. As I slogged through the mud at the barn, I saw a friend's horse, Killian, standing in his pen and taking in the first sunlight he'd seen in days. His ears perked up as he watched me walk toward him. I intuitively asked him how the rainy week had been for him, expecting him to say it was cold and dreary. Instead, Killian responded enthusiastically, "All the water was falling from the sky!"

If we approach each experience with fresh eyes, noticing the magic of everything that life has to offer, we can see things differently. For a week, I'd been complaining with my barn mates about when the rain would end. Killian, on the other hand, marveled at the fact that the water was coming from above instead of merely sitting in his water bucket. His curiosity was infectious, and I found myself splashing in a few puddles with childlike glee as I returned to my car.

Embrace the Blessings

Marlboro stood in the pasture as I approached him; I immediately became aware of a knee injury. I asked his owner about it, and her eyes filled with tears as she acknowledged that a jumping accident the year before had damaged his knee and ended his jumping career. I asked Marlboro about it, expecting him to express dismay about his injury. To my surprise, he happily announced, "I'm retired!" He showed me days spent grazing in green pastures, rolling in the grass, and feeling the warm sun on his back.

Unlike his owner, who lamented that his path was cut short, Marlboro saw only a life filled with the joys of simply being a horse without having to work. He fully accepted his life, embracing his experience and making the most of it. If we can find a way to embrace whatever comes, we too can feel the peace and calm of just living for the moment, enjoying the blessings available to us, and not giving a thought to "what might have been."

Those Who Truly Love You Won't Hurt You

Dehli was a fiery chestnut red mare. Her pinned ears told me that entrance to her stall was by invitation only; I had to ask her if I could talk to her. She described her life with princess flair; she wanted the treats she liked, the hay she preferred, and the free time she coveted. Dehli's owner said she was a challenge to ride, and she wasn't sure if Dehli actually liked her. I asked Dehli how she felt, and Dehli answered me with a sassy attitude as she said, "I could spin around and dump her any time I want to, but I'm not going to." I asked her why not, and Dehli said, "Because I love her."

Relationships aren't always easy, and letting yourself be vulnerable can be a challenge. Opening ourselves up to another means giving them the power to hurt us. And yet, when we love someone, we choose not to hurt them even though we could. Those who choose to hurt us don't deserve further access to us. Those who truly love us will protect our tender hearts.

Be Present with the Ones You Love

Remington was a majestic gray horse, standing tall and proud in his stall as he gazed at me with piercing eyes. He informed me that he was a talented jumper and described the ribbons he'd won at various horse shows. I asked him about his partnership with his owner, and he told me they were a "regal pair." He then admitted that one show had not gone well. He told me that his owner usually connects deeply with him right before they go into the show ring, but she was distracted at that show and didn't do so. Unfortunately, they weren't listening to each other, and they fell over one of the fences.

It's important to be present and make true connections with those around us. Our companions deserve our full focus. In a world that seems to get faster every day, multi-tasking our relationships prevents us from experiencing the richness they have to offer. When we are deeply present with others, we can truly take in every moment.

Set Boundaries to Prioritize Your Self-Care

Rogue was a spicy Thoroughbred mare who hopped and bucked around show ring fences as often as she jumped them. A quiet and shy teenaged girl loved Rogue deeply and bravely tolerated her shenanigans, until Rogue wheeled away from a jump so hard that her owner flew into the dirt and broke her tailbone. I asked Rogue why she made things so challenging for her owner, and she said, "That's what I'm here for." I asked her to explain, and Rogue said, "When she learns to take charge with me, she'll take charge with everyone else, too."

It is one thing to set boundaries with those who hurt us, but it is far more challenging to set boundaries with our loved ones. When we care about someone else, we are less inclined to take care of ourselves. However, when we prioritize ourselves as well, we honor our needs by setting clear standards about what we will allow into our lives, which also strengthens our relationships with others.

Release Your Past Trauma and Focus on Gratitude

Troy was dirt-encrusted, bony, and forgotten until a caring and committed horse lover saved him from a trailer headed to slaughter and gave him a happy home. She asked me if I could pick up any information about Troy's past. As I connected with him, I anticipated stories of darkness, but was pleasantly surprised to feel a burst of energy filled with warm golden light. I asked him to tell me about his life, and he said, "I have the *best* life!" He talked of the love his owner had shown him, his delicious food and treats, and his stall filled with fluffy shavings where he liked to nap. He had no negative memories to share and no grudges to hold.

It can be incredibly challenging to let go of the wounds we've suffered, and our "stories" are often filled with the difficulties we've overcome and the pain we've experienced. And yet, if we can turn our attention to the beauty in our lives, the happiness we've felt, and the love we've shared, we can change those stories. When we focus on our blessings, we fill our lives with gratitude and joy, which brings even more of it into our lives.

Animals have incredible depth and wisdom. When we take the time to listen to what they have to say, the opportunities for growth and compassion—for them as well as for ourselves—are endless.

Bio

Karen Gabler is an award-winning attorney, intuitive mentor, psychic medium, animal communicator and Reiki master. She also is a best-selling author, teacher, and inspirational speaker. Karen is passionate about encouraging others to find their highest purpose and live their best lives. She mentors her clients through a variety of personal and business issues, marrying her practical legal and business experience with her innate intuitive ability to receive information and guidance from higher sources. She also facilitates connections with clients' loved ones in spirit. Karen conducts workshops and presentations on a variety of business, spiritual and personal development topics. She earned her Bachelor of Arts in psychology from the University of Hawaii and her Juris Doctorate from the William S. Richardson School of Law at the University of Hawaii. Karen has pursued wide-ranging education in interpersonal development and the spiritual sciences, working with tutors from the prestigious Arthur Findlay College for the Psychic Sciences in England as well as with numerous intuitives and mediums throughout the United States. She is a WCIT in the Martha Beck Wayfinder life coaching program. Karen enjoys reading, hiking, horseback riding and spending time with her husband and two children. You can find Karen at www.karengabler.com.

Chapter Seven
Returning the Favor
By Sarah Gabler

As a child, I took riding lessons on a variety of leased ponies owned by my English riding trainer. Their names were Ruby, Tag, Cheeto, Rawley, and Casey. I didn't technically "own" them, but I took care of them and rode them regularly. I loved each of these ponies like they were my own, and I loved the responsibility of taking care of such sweet animals. I rode every Saturday morning in the ring with my mother while she rode her own horse, Jupiter. I loved Jupiter like I loved my leased horses, but he was much bigger and more powerful than I could manage, so our interactions were limited to feeding him cookies after my mom's lesson.

Jupiter was a handful for my mother. He was a good boy, but he had his fair share of funny and quirky moments. From bucks to spins to sprints across the ring, my mother had to be ready for anything at any time. I didn't think I would ever be able to ride him. To my surprise, on a beautiful summer day at the barn, my trainer turned to my mother and said, "I think Sarah's ready to get on Jupiter." I was so excited! I could see the doubt on my mother's face, but she trusted our trainer's judgment. My father helped me lift the saddle onto Jupiter's back, towering above me. As I put my helmet on, my mother walked up to Jupiter and took his muzzle in her hands. He held her gaze as she looked deeply into his eyes and said, "Please, Jupiter, take care of my baby!"

Despite his history of silly moments with my mother, taking care of me is exactly what Jupiter did. He instantly became a quiet spirit, standing completely still as my trainer boosted me onto his back. He walked slowly while I clutched the reins and became used to his much larger steps. He waited patiently until I was ready to ask him to trot, then stepped slowly into a faster gait only after I sat up and pushed my heels down in my stirrups. He never ran off with me, never spun, and never bucked. If he spooked at something, the most he would do is make a tiny hop to the side to lean away from a dangerous bush or swaying tree branch.

Jupiter became so calm that even my mother couldn't believe he was the same horse she had ridden for years. His canter was smooth and controlled, his small jumps were gentle and easy, and I was having the time of my life! I learned so much about working with a larger animal, trusting him to listen to me and making sure that I listened to him as well. Over the next few years, I developed such a special connection with Jupiter. He learned to accept the guidance from my small legs, and I learned that he would make sure we got over obstacles safely. Outside of the ring, I would hang out in his stall and pet him while he munched on his hay and cookies. I felt a connection that was much greater than anything I had experienced before, and spending time with Jupiter quickly became my favorite part of the week.

As I transitioned into middle school, my relationship with Jupiter continued to deepen and became more and more special to me. After a day of pre-teen bullying or when I was feeling alone, spending time with Jupiter made me forget about my problems and recognize that there were still others who cared deeply about me and loved me just as I am. I gained a much deeper understanding of what it meant to have an animal become a best friend.

I was growing as a rider and as a person, and Jupiter was enjoying working with me and taking things slowly. As our lessons continued, I was excited about our progress. I became older and grew taller. My confidence grew, and Jupiter and I began to jump higher fences and longer courses. We had so much fun together!

Several years into our lessons, I began to see gray hairs in Jupiter's mane and realized something I hadn't focused on previously: Jupiter was growing older as well. One morning, my trainer and my mother initiated a "group meeting" before my lesson. They were hesitant and I was worried that there was something wrong with Jupiter, but my mother and trainer assured me he was fine. They explained to me that Jupiter was getting into his senior years and slowing down. To protect his health, he would need to jump smaller jumps, and jump less often. They told me that if I wanted to keep progressing into more competitive riding, I wouldn't be able to do it with Jupiter.

I didn't have a moment's hesitation in knowing that slowing down was completely fine with me. I had learned through my years of riding with Jupiter that the connection we had didn't come from how fast we went or how high I jumped. It came from the time I spent with him and the fun we had together. I thought about how he kept me safe when I was so young and my abilities were limited, and how he made sure I was completely safe while waiting for me to catch up with him. I thought about how my mother asked him to take care of me and recognized that it was now time for me to take care of him. I wrapped my arms around him as I told my mother and trainer that it didn't bother me at all that Jupiter wasn't going to jump super high: I was happy just spending time with him.

For the next few years, I reduced our speed and lowered our jumps to make sure that Jupiter was comfortable. I put salve on his legs and gave him massages and warm baths. My top priority was making sure that he was happy, healthy, and safe. In return, he continued to give me everything he could in every lesson. Taking it easy and giving him extra care made it possible for him to be strong and fit to this day. We still ride every Saturday and Jupiter is feeling great—often, he chooses to jump a little higher than necessary, showing us that he's "still got it!" He is energetic and happy, and I couldn't be more fulfilled by working with him and spending time with him before and after our lesson as we did before.

I feel blessed to be able to return the favor Jupiter gave to me. He met me where I was when I was a child, even though he had to limit his playfulness and control his outbursts. He accepted what I could do and let me find my way with his loving guidance. In return, I have met him where he is as well, allowing him to decide what he feels capable of handling on any given day and rewarding his efforts with extra tender loving care. I've learned through this experience that when you love someone and care for them as much as Jupiter and I love and care for each other, nothing you do is a sacrifice. Instead, it's a gift, and it will be more fulfilling than you ever could've imagined.

Bio

Sarah Gabler is 17 years old and is a senior in high school. She adores spending time with her family and traveling to new places. Sarah loves playing ukulele, guitar, and keyboard, and riding or spending time with her horse. Sarah is a lifelong artist and loves using creative outlets to express herself. She is an internationally best-selling author and has contributed her work to multiple published collections of short stories with As You Wish Publishing. She works as a stage manager for her school productions, and loves bringing shows to life to entertain others. Sarah plans to major in psychology at the University of Oregon and wants to study abroad during her college years. She began exploring spiritual teachings, self-development, and soul empowerment concepts when she was just 10 years old and believes it has made her a better person today. It has motivated her to pursue her best life as well as to help others on their fulfillment journey. Sarah wants to empower people by helping them recognize their true potential. She believes that even the smallest acts of kindness can make someone's day, and she always tries her best to help others feel heard, seen, and loved.

Chapter Eight
Monkey: The Dog Who Changed My Life
By Dr. Sushma D.A. Hallock

We were living in Calgary, Alberta, Canada when a single bad experience made me afraid of dogs. My mom dropped us off at my grandmother's house before work, and we stayed there until we went to school. Our school was on the north corner of an open grassy field, and there was a small hill between the school and a soccer field. Grannie lived about a ten-minute walk south of our elementary school. Instead of using the sidewalk on the school's east side, I walked through the field.

On a typical Calgary winter day, which meant it was below 0°C, I was wearing my blue snowsuit and a long brown scarf as I used the shortcut through the field. There were other kids in the field. I then noticed a large dog (as a petite West Indian female, I'm sure everything at that time seemed big back then) coming toward me and began to bark at me. I froze. I did not grow up with animals or have any experience with them and their behavior. As a result, I had no clue if it was a 'hello' bark or a 'hey, stay out of my way' bark. I just stood there, paralyzed. I didn't know if it was a stray or a family pet of one of the kids in the field; it didn't matter. I was petrified. Then, as quickly as the dog appeared, it left. Bottom line—I was never the same after that. I would experience panic whenever I saw a dog, even if the owner said the dog was friendly. As I got older, I never considered having any pet with four legs. I thought, what if I get bitten? What if I get scratched? My fear led me to imagine the worst.

Years later, I moved away from Canada to pursue graduate school in Boston, Massachusetts, USA, where I met and married my amazing husband (you can read more in "Manifesting the Love of My Life" in my collaborative book *Awaken Your Magic*). Kevin was a 6'5" farm boy from Michigan; he grew up around every farm animal imaginable: chickens, ducks, sheep, dogs, cats, goats, and the occasional cow! I was still scared of having a pet even though my loving husband reassured me that I would be fine. As the years passed and our quest for a family proved unsuccessful, I turned my attention to my academic and spiritual training.

I became a spiritual student under the tutelage of Tony Stockwell. I first met Tony at Journey Within, a well-known Spiritualist church in New Jersey. From there on, I developed and strengthened my skills as an intuitive medium; I could communicate with people who crossed over to the other side. Little did I know that Tony was an animal communicator and passionate about animals! Intuitively, I was drawn to people who loved animals, while I feared them. In June 2020, I started my formal training in a branch of mediumship called Trance Mediumship. Tony described it as an altered state of consciousness that allows a blending of souls for channeling guidance. He taught us how to develop and control it.

We were encouraged to practice weekly, and I was fortunate to work with a phenomenal group of women! These women were skilled intuitive practitioners, and because of them, I would meditate every day to improve my skills. Ironically, my trance training unlocked my hidden skills as an animal communicator! I chuckle at this—the West Indian woman who grew up afraid of dogs can now communicate with them? Truth is stranger than fiction! After every practice session, I had a habit of calling my fellow trance medium, Stacy C. (who eventually became one of my best friends and a trusted mentor), to connect and unwind. One evening, as I was chatting with her, I had a "feeling" about her dogs. I started sharing the intuitive thoughts coming through for Lola and Monkey. Lola was a Chihuahua and Rat Terrier mix, while Monkey was a Chihuahua and Miniature

Pinscher mix. She had another Chihuahua named Howie; his nickname was Professor Howie, but he had crossed over the Rainbow Bridge before I met Stacy.

I was drawn to Monkey. There was something about him that I could not resist. I was able to tap into his spirit easily. I knew things about his personality, habits, likes, and dislikes, which only Stacy could validate. Stacy is a natural animal communicator and has worked with other animal communicators, so it was a surprise for both of us that I was able to do this. Monkey changed my life—he became my animal communicator teacher on earth and helped me hone my skills!

After this eureka moment, I took a leap of faith. With Stacy's encouragement, I started offering free readings via Zoom for pet parents—I did gallery readings, 1-to-1s, and email readings. It was at the end of my first gallery reading in July 2020 that someone asked me if I could read horses (during the gallery, I was able to connect with her dog, Ripple). I told her that I didn't know but was willing to try!

In August of that summer, I read for Star—her favorite horse. It was another monumental moment in my life. Before I met Star, I took some time to review the anatomy of a horse; again, I was listening to my intuition and going with the flow. We had a fantastic session! Intuitively connecting to Star was like connecting to an old friend! I could share things with Jules about Star that she knew and other things that she did not. Jules was incredibly kind, patient, and willing to work with me for several weeks, bolstering my skills on reading different animals. I read for Donnie the goat and Jimmy the sheep, Twix the pig, followed by a mini donkey! We even did a trance reading for her horse, Feisty. This session validated that I could connect intuitively with horses very easily.

Because of Monkey, Stacy, and Jules, I established myself within the intuitive community as an animal communicator, which allowed me to work with people from England, Australia, Sweden, and Holland, to mention a few countries. With Tony's guidance, he recommended that I become The Rainbow Bridge Medium. Before becoming an animal communicator—I was unable to understand the depths of people's emotional connections with their fur babies.

I remember the day Stacy told me that Monkey had passed. It was like someone had ripped my heart out. I cried like I had never cried before. The sadness I felt was overwhelming. Even though I had never had a chance to hold Monkey or to play with him, I felt like he was my fur baby, too. I was Auntie Sush, and I would have done anything for him. And I loved him and still love him with all my heart!

I am very thankful for the lessons I've learned from Monkey and all the other fur babies I've been privileged to connect with. They have taught me to love unconditionally and to have fun in the here and now. Interestingly, Monkey, Professor Howie, and Lola have all chosen to be a part of my spiritual team. I will be forever grateful—thank you, Monkey!

Bio

My name is Dr. Sushma D.A. Hallock. I was born in Guyana, South America; I identify as both West Indian and South Asian. My parents moved to Canada when I was very young—we lived in Calgary, Alberta and then Toronto, Ontario. I eventually moved to Boston, Massachusetts, for graduate school. This is where I got married, completed a Master's in Anatomy & Neurobiology, an MBA, and finally finished my doctoral work in Clinical Sexology with a focus on Sex Education in the fall of 2023. During my quest of self-discovery, I participated in intuitive courses with Tony Stockwell, Ann Theato, and many more intuitive practitioners. I see myself as a voracious learner and an intuitive artist. I can connect with people on an intellectual level and on a soul-to-soul level. Along my spiritual journey of self-discovery, I learned that

I am an animal whisperer and can communicate with animals, both present and with those who have crossed over to the other side. I embraced my new skills and eventually became The Rainbow Bridge Medium (www.therainbowbridgemedium.com). I feel incredibly blessed to know my purpose in life—to help every being have a voice!

Chapter Nine
Faith Creates Miracles
By Erica Hess

One cold day in the winter of 2017, Stephanie, the executive director of New Mexico Equine Rescue, came out for a visit. After touring the ranch, she asked if she might be able to see me work with a horse. So, I brought Yogi out of the barn and down to the round pen. We conversed lightly as I brought this huge guy in, but when I began the session, the air became quite still. Yogi and I moved as one around the rim of the pen in our initial "friendship walk." Our feet hit the sand in a unified cadence and then we began to move in circles, twirling in patterns together, then apart, then back together. It was a beautiful "dance." Stephanie was amazed that I never put a lead rope around Yogi's neck. She said, "He was just stuck to you like some kind of invisible glue." Then she asked, "What is he like to ride?" I answered, "Aah, we don't ride this horse." She looked down at us in the pen and her eyes were more curious now. I said, "He doesn't want to be ridden."

As the three of us walked back to the barn, Stephanie

paused. She touched my sleeve and asked if I was willing to work with one of the horses from her horse rescue. She had a "special guy" that needed help. I asked her why this horse, out of the nearly 50 horses that she cares for? "There's just something about him," she offered. "He's been through several trainers already, but no one seems to get him, so we keep pulling him back out of training."

I hesitated for a few reasons: one is that we knew we would have to charge for our time to work with this horse, even though they were a non-profit. Another is that the horse had already been through several training programs with little success. What, I wondered, were we going to be able to give him that no one else could? We were really curious about this horse because of her insistence and finally agreed to take him for a few months.

Paddy arrived on a bitterly cold day in November. A handsome sorrel with a thick white blaze down the center of his face. Maybe something like a quarter horse-draft cross, with the broadest chest I'd ever seen. Strong, stoic, and deeply braced against the world.

Every once in a while, we meet a horse who seems to be just out of reach, a bit aloof and extremely present at the same time, and they are always more intense than the others. But they possess a quality—a depth and an air of confidence about them; they seem to carry themselves with such authority that the other horses naturally take heed of them. They may live along the outskirts of the herd, but when they choose to enter, the herd will part ways and make room for them inside the group. They don't have to push their way in or fight their way to the top. This is certainly not the norm, and we believe that this shows the herd's respect and acceptance of the new horse. They seem to know he is special.

Paddy began his training with us that day. It took several weeks to get a halter on him and many more to begin formal training since touching him was out of the question. In regular sessions, he remained aloof and braced. We worked so patiently with him doing very basic horsemanship sessions and even had him under saddle for brief moments. But we always felt that Paddy could explode at any moment. One thing was clear; this horse was not yet adoptable. Sadly, our friends at the horse rescue decided to take him out of training. Ouch. This was a special guy, and we had already made such a commitment to him. We resolved to adopt him and continue his rehabilitation.

We stopped his formal "training" because we felt that he needed more time to let go of his trauma. With a call for help, many people donated money so we could keep him here. We made him a promise that he could stay here forever and that he could take as long as he needed to trust us, if ever.

That spring, we went to France to work with our mentors, Frederic Pignon and Magali Delgado. At the end of a glorious week with them I asked Fred for his advice with Paddy. We already understood that we had to give up everything we had done so far and start over. We asked about how to "work" with him. Fred answered, "No, no, no. You cannot work with him yet. He's not ready for that." And that's when it all began to change.

We gave Paddy a primo paddock in one of the barns where he could live alone but surrounded by the herd. Every day, I would walk into his paddock, my pockets stuffed with treats, which would spill carelessly out of my shorts as I mucked about in there. I would ignore him entirely except for an occasional sideways glance in order to spy on his reactions. Each time I returned, he would be a bit more curious. Some days, I pulled up a chair to nap in the corner. I didn't engage or try to touch him. Eventually, he began following me around, waiting for delicious things to fall in my wake.

Slowly (so painfully slowly), I introduced a bucket of grain on my lap for him to eat from. This is how we "worked" for many months. Every once in a while, as he ate grain from the bucket, his cheek would graze my hand. After another long while, I reintroduced his halter and lead rope. I began a new courtship with him while I tried to click the rope on and off.

Eventually, I could lead him outside to the 'cookie jar' without any persuasion. At some point, by necessity, we had to move him into our main paddock with five other horses. The backslide happened so fast we couldn't believe our eyes. He just withdrew so suddenly.

He was distant from us again. It seemed like he felt rejected. Our beautiful, intimate, long, slow dance had abruptly ended, and we couldn't find each other. We were both heartbroken.

After all these months, I was at the end of my rope. I lost all hope and thought we had failed. I felt, for the first time, that he was never going to trust us or anyone, and I wondered if I could really believe in our work.

My husband, Joost, never let me believe there was no hope. My best friend told me how her teenage daughters would backslide all the time while growing up. I gritted my teeth, let go of my expectations, and started over.

Then COVID happened. We were ordered to shelter at home. And I suddenly had a whole lot more time to be with him. So, I just sat in his paddock while he ate or slept. And I waited. We took walks. We played together in the arenas. The truth is, I had grown incredibly fond of him.

When we needed to move the horses around, I made the decision to try again to bring Paddy out with the others into the main paddock. It was time to try something new. He watched me intensely as I tentatively took off the halter. He stood with me for a moment instead of running away. I lowered my head, said a prayer, and left the barn.

First thing the next morning, he was waiting at the gate when I walked in. He approaches me now to be haltered. He stands by the gate, looking out with soft eyes, hoping for a visit from me or one of our clients.

My own lessons with Paddy are becoming clear now; my expectations and my plan were inspired and informed by my personal experience. But when my plan didn't work as expected, I felt I had to give up. In fact, it was precisely when I surrendered that the magic began to happen. Paddy was now mine!

Faith is not the same thing as knowledge, even though they are both learned. Faith creates miracles.

Horses have the skill to mirror hope and revive the spirit of those who have been broken by abuse, negligence and hardship.

Bio

Erica lives in Santa Fe, NM, with her husband, Joost, and their herd of 14 horses. Both Erica and Joost are in long-term recovery from SUD. Avid horse-people, and advocates for horses and recovery, they started the non-profit, "A Chance of a Lifetime," to rescue and rehab neglected horses. At COLT, humans and horses recover together, offering hope and healing to many who suffer from trauma and SUD. www.achanceofalifetime.org

Chapter Ten
Bridge of Discovery: My Parkway Journey
By Marnie Hollander

Nevele, affectionately known as Nev, was a cherished Maltese-Poodle mix and my beloved heart dog, who brought boundless joy and companionship into my world. Our adventures and enduring memories were a testament to our deep bond. However, as fate would have it, Nev fell ill with Cushing's disease, a condition that slowly drained his vitality.

I did everything possible to help him, consulted with the best veterinarians, and explored various treatment options. However, as time went on, it became clear that the disease was taking its toll. The once-vibrant dog was now weak and miserable. The difficult decision to put him down had to be made, and my heart shattered into a million pieces.

After saying the final goodbyes to my 13-year-old pup, I was in a sea of grief. The emptiness in my home was overwhelming, and I longed for a way to heal my broken heart. As fall approached, I heard whispers of the breathtaking beauty of the leaves in North Carolina. Determined to find solace and a sense of renewal, I embarked on a journey to witness this natural wonder.

Driving through the picturesque Blue Ridge Parkway, I marveled at the vibrant red, orange, and gold hues that painted the landscape. The winding roads mirror the twists and turns of my own life, and I found comfort in the serenity of nature. A sudden change of direction led me to notice the Lake Lure Flowering Bridge sign, sparking my curiosity. Despite my interest, I hesitated to explore further due to safety concerns on the busy road. Deciding to research the location online later, I had no idea that this choice would ultimately lead me to a significant revelation.

Upon returning to the hotel in the evening, I began researching the fascinating history of the Lake Lure Flowering Bridge. This bridge, formerly a highway, had been transformed into a beautiful garden filled with colorful flowers and lush greenery. However, the most captivating discovery was a secluded path within the garden—the Rainbow Bridge. Looking at the Rainbow Bridge pictures, I couldn't help but feel emotional. Until then, I had only considered it a mythical place where pets went after they died. People believed it was a paradise where pets played and waited for their human companions to join them one day. As I continued scrolling, I realized that I would have walked the path to the real-life Rainbow Bridge had I visited the Flowering Bridge Garden. A real place where those who had lost their pets could leave mementos such as collars, leashes, and photographs to honor their memories.

The thought of standing at the threshold of that sacred place, surrounded by the tokens of love left by others, overwhelmed me.

At that moment, I experienced a mix of relief and regret. I was relieved not to have encountered the Rainbow Bridge during my brief detour at the Flowering Bridge, as it would have reopened the wound of losing Nev. Yet, I also regretted not being able to leave a token of remembrance at the Rainbow Bridge.

Determined to honor Nev's memory and find closure, I returned to North Carolina and fulfilled my desire to leave a small piece of Nev at the Rainbow Bridge. It became my mission to find comfort and healing in this symbolic act of remembrance.

Over time, my plan began to form. I gathered photographs of Nev, carefully selecting those that reflected his essence and our affection. I opted to bring his first stuffed animal, Snoopy, as a keepsake to leave at the bridge. With this memento, I started my journey back to North Carolina.

As I stood at the entrance of the Flowering Bridge, I took a deep breath. The air was crisp, and the blooming flowers filled my senses. I walked along the bridge, taking in the beauty that surrounded me. The vibrant colors reflected the memories I held dear, reminding me of the joy Nev brought to my life.

Finally, I reached the end of the Flowering Bridge, where a small path led to the Rainbow Bridge. I hesitated momentarily, my heart pounding with a mix of emotions. With each step I took, I felt a sense of peace. The weight of grief began to lift, replaced by a profound connection to Nev and the countless others who had crossed over the Rainbow Bridge.

Numerous symbols of affection decorated the space, each representing the deep connection between people and their animal companions. I added Nev's pictures, Snoopy toy, and collar to the display, experiencing closure and appreciation.

At that instant, I understood that the Rainbow Bridge held significance beyond its physical presence; it symbolized the everlasting relationship between humans and their cherished pets. It served as a reminder that love knows no bounds and that the memories of our departed loved ones will always be treasured.

With a heavy heart but also a newfound sense of peace, I turned to leave the Rainbow Bridge. As I walked back, I couldn't help but smile. Nev's spirit will always be with me, guiding me through life's twists and turns.

From that day forward, I carried the memory of Nev in my heart, finding comfort in the beauty of nature and the knowledge that our bond would never be broken. As I continue my journey through life, I vowed to honor Nev's memory by spreading love and kindness to all, as he had done for me.

And so, my story became a testament to the power of love, loss, and the healing that can be found in unexpected places. The Flowering Bridge and the Rainbow Bridge had now intertwined, guiding me toward acceptance and a renewed sense of purpose. As I drove away, I knew I would forever hold my Nevele close, carrying his spirit with me on every new adventure.

Bio

Marnie Hollander, a devoted mother to two young adults and two dogs, cherishes her visits to Colorado to spend time with her children. In addition to creating multimedia art and graphic design, she takes pleasure in nurturing her plant collection and assisting her loved ones with their projects. She also appreciates music, sports, sunsets, and the mountains. Marnie is excited to share this story, representing a significant milestone in her creative journey.

"I spent every weekend with those horses for several months. We had both been through our own traumas and gradually healed together...Day after day, they stood patiently as I brushed their coats and poured out my heart. The ability to share with them my deepest sorrows without the fear of judgment was priceless. Over time, I realized that those horses had done more to help me than I could ever do to help them."

Amy I King

Chapter Eleven
From Heartbreak to Hoofbeats
By Amy I King

"I'm starting a new professional adventure. A group has rescued 17 horses from a terribly abusive situation, and I have been hired to work with them. I will be looking for volunteers to help me with them." I couldn't believe my ears as I listened to one of the women in our cabin tell me and my cabin mates about this fantastic opportunity. A few months after a devastating breakup, I was on a weekend church retreat with a friend and her mother in the foothills. I had always wanted to work with horses, and my empathic heart was immediately captivated. Having recently survived the almost unbearable heartbreak of coming home from work one day to find my live-in boyfriend and all of his belongings gone without a trace, I was broken. My heart fell into my stomach as I approached the closet to find his clothing gone.

I had no clue he would leave me when I dropped him at the bus stop that morning and kissed him, telling him to have a great day. Things would have been different if I had known it would be the last kiss. We had what I believed was a good thing. I would drop him at the bus stop, where he would ride to work, and I would go on to my job. In the afternoons, I would go home briefly after work to let my dog out and then pick him up at his job. The security guard shouted at my car that afternoon, "He didn't come to work today." My heart began to beat hard and fast as I raced home. That experience left me feeling abandoned and broken. Looking back 20 years later with the wisdom I have now, I realize that our relationship burned hard and fast, never good if you want it to last, and his attachment style was avoidant; therefore, it was only a matter of time before he was off to the next woman. When he and I met, I had recently been dumped by a man whom I cared for when he met and later married a woman in Europe. Rebound can be a disaster when you just want to be loved and don't know how to love yourself. He would never fully commit to me, and it's entirely possible that I was being used for a place to live. I later learned that while I would go to bed early, he was on the computer chatting with his next conquest in Texas, where he headed when he left my house. He was a wanderer, and I just wanted to be loved. Heartbroken, I needed something other than my job as a revenue analyst on which to focus my attention. Working with horses would be a great way to help me heal and give back to a good cause.

I could see the property on which the horses were housed from my apartment, making the commute a breeze. From day one, I was thrilled to be surrounded by these forgiving animals. I could see the sadness in their eyes, and their mistrust of humans was evident. After all, they had been starved, left without water, and abused for much of their lives. These 17 survivors were the lucky ones. Seven others didn't make it out of the abuser's hands alive, their carcasses found by the Sheriff on the property of their now-incarcerated abuser.

When I started with the organization, Beth, the rescuer, had me working inside the house doing clerical work. I called celebrities or their assistants, explained what we were doing, and asked for generous donations. I was also in charge of mailing information packets out to as many influential people as possible, working each day from a pile of pages containing addresses. I was disappointed with my station when Beth asked if I would be interested in being hands-on with the horses. "Yes!" Quickly sprung from my lips. It had been several weeks, and I was waiting for the opportunity.

I was responsible for working with the three beautiful mini horses and developed quite an affinity for one in particular, Buttercup. She was a lovely beige and white female with the most innocent and soulful eyes. One of the most beautiful things about horses and animals is the pure love and lack of judgment bestowed upon their caretakers. They are such forgiving creatures.

Every weekend, I would wake up, care for my dog & cat, and make my way over to the property adjacent to Beth's home where the horses were being kept. I looked forward to weekends more than I had in a long while. I had a purpose that filled my heart with immense joy. I no longer spent weekends crying over what I had thought I had lost; I spent it loving on the most amazing creatures on earth.

Day after day, I would brush the minis, talking to them and getting them accustomed to being around someone in a wheelchair. The organization's ultimate goal was to use the horses as therapy for youth with physical challenges. The horses grew more trusting each day, letting their guard down gradually. And each day, my heart softened a little more, healing the scars left by my ex-boyfriend, a man whom I trusted with my whole heart. I was also broadening my community. The family who had taken in the horses welcomed me and the other volunteers into their daily lives.

One day, as I was brushing Buttercup and giving her kisses, she made a mistake and caught her leg between the widely spaced graphite spokes of the wheel of my wheelchair. She panicked and dragged my chair for about 10 feet before stopping. I gently reached down and guided her hoof from between the spokes, and she let out a neigh. The trust was building.

I spent every weekend with those horses for several months. We had both been through our own traumas and gradually healed together. I looked forward to every moment I could spend with "my minis" as we began to build a strong relationship. Day after day, they stood patiently as I brushed their coats and poured out my heart. The ability to share with them my deepest sorrows without the fear of judgment was priceless. Over time, I realized that those horses had done more to help me than I could ever do to help them.

Soon, I could feel my heart had healed. No longer did I wake with the pain of sadness and loss. Research has shown that interacting with horses has many benefits, including decreased stress levels, lower blood pressure, and reduced feelings of anger, hostility, tension, and depression.

I woke each morning with a vigor and a zest for life again. My confidence was building with each day spent among the horses. I returned to my old self, largely thanks to my work with those majestic beings.

I have learned that the universe will put opportunities for growth and healing into our paths, always at the right time. Our only obligation is to say yes to what feels right within our souls. I am grateful that Jan, the community, and the opportunity to work with the horses were put in my path 20 years ago; our time together has been one of the hallmarks of my life thus far.

Bio

Amy I King is a Certified Life Coach/owner of Your Phenomenal Life, LLC. She is the best-selling author of *Messy Wheels: Stories From Where I Sit* and contributing author of international best sellers: *Inspirations: 101 Uplifting Stories for Daily Happiness, Manifestations: True Stories of Bringing the Imagined into Reality, The Grateful Soul: The Art and Practice of Gratitude, The Courageous Heart: Finding Strength in Difficult Times, Ordinary Oneness, Enduring Wisdom, 365 Days of Self Love, Whispers from the Heart, Wisdom Keepers*, and many more. When not writing, she enjoys improv classes, cardio drumming, music, movies, art, meditation, travel, and time spent with her chosen family.

Amy has overcome many challenges from which she draws wisdom to assist clients. Amy's greatest joy is using her experiences to help others move past their personal blocks and outdated beliefs to become empowered to live their dreams. Every challenge, she believes, is put before us to enable us to evolve and grow into the highest version of ourselves.

She builds relationships with clients based on trust and vulnerability. She welcomes the opportunity to help you transform your life!

Email her at Amy.kinglifecoaching@gmail.com

Chapter Twelve

Princess's Odyssey: A Tale of Love Healing Pain

By Dr. Sally Nazari

For many of us, there's a furry, feathered, or finned companion that we consider part of our family. Whether it's a cat curling up in our lap, a bird chirping in its aviary, or a fish swimming gracefully in its tank, our hearts warm at the mere thought of them. Their presence brings us comfort and solace, particularly during stressful times, and we're often amazed by how effortlessly they brighten our days.

Research suggests that many animals have an innate knack for connecting with others, often making them impeccable pets. Moreover, many of these animals go on to become adept healers through their innate traits. Pets who provide a unique comfort for those they live with are referred to as Emotional Support Animals, or ESAs. Pets who serve as ESAs differ from service animals in that they are not trained to assist with struggles in any specific way, yet their presence and interactions do offer assistance that can facilitate healing and recovery for their human companions.

One way animals provide emotional support is by helping increase oxytocin levels. Oxytocin is beneficial because it slows heart rate, lowers blood pressure, and helps prevent stress hormone production. Therefore, elevated levels of this hormone in the body can promote feelings of calmness and peace. This chemical alone can assist in combating the negative emotions and mental health effects often experienced following trauma. Scientific observation supports an increase in the release of this so-called 'happiness' chemical as a result of animal interaction.

Pets can also assist us in letting go of feelings of anger and resentment, which are often experienced by individuals who have faced trauma. These emotions can be some of the most challenging to overcome in the aftermath of trauma. However, releasing them can have a lasting positive impact on mental health. Many individuals seek support from mental health professionals to reach a place where they can let go of these and other related feelings. Pets, unlike humans, do not hold onto these emotions, and their companionship may enable many people to shed anger and resentment more easily.

Cats and other pets that offer emotional support can also assist us in learning how to remain mindful and present in the moment. The practice of mindfulness brings various benefits, including improved time management, enhanced mood, and increased emotional stability. While mindfulness can be beneficial for anyone, it holds particular significance for individuals who have experienced trauma. For them, practicing mindfulness becomes an essential tool for stress relief and coping with the aftermath of trauma.

The significant impact of pets on our well-being is evident in how many of us feel instantly better at the mere thought of spending time with our interspecies loved ones. In fact, numerous individuals report missing their pets as much, if not more, than other family members. This deep emotional connection stems from the support and comfort that pets offer, particularly during challenging times such as anxiety, depression, or the aftermath of trauma.

Although exposure to traumatic events can lead to various psychological effects that are often challenging to overcome, many individuals find solace and happiness by actively working through them. Living with a pet can greatly facilitate and expedite this process, as pet ownership provides constant companionship, structure, and affection. Moreover, beyond these immediate benefits, our pets can also impart valuable life lessons. In fact, numerous individuals who previously felt helpless after experiencing trauma reported experiencing disproportionately high benefits from living with an adopted pet afterward, even when considering the additional costs associated with pet ownership. While living with an animal may not be suitable for everyone, individuals who currently have pets or are considering adopting one should weigh the myriad benefits animal companions can offer. In my own life, I've experienced the priceless joy of forming deep connections with many animals.

On the heels of this information, please allow me to introduce Princess, a beautiful house panther with black fur as soft as silk. Her story is not one of a carefree feline existence but rather a journey that began with abandonment, injury, and trauma. Rescued from the wilderness as a kitten, Princess was abandoned as a newborn by her mother, leading to a nervous system impairment. She once bore the scars of her past both physically and emotionally, evident in her cautious demeanor and wary eyes that told of a youth filled with hardship and fear.

In the quiet corners of our lives, where the mundane often reigns, there exists a profound source of inspiration that can emerge unexpectedly. Princess's tale is one such inspiring example, highlighting the transformative and healing influence of love and courage. It indeed parallels Homer's Odyssey in exemplifying journey and transformation, resilience and perseverance after trauma, and finding peace and love in the face of hardship. Princess's story begins with a seemingly ordinary feral cat, but within the depths of her golden eyes lies a tale of resilience, loyalty, companionship, and the transformative power of love.

Despite her troubling past, Princess eventually found herself in a home filled with love and compassion. Her previous environment, marked by carelessness and neglect, failed to meet her need for attentiveness and thoughtfulness. After enduring months of turmoil and carelessness, Princess's internal wounds manifested outwardly. She suffered a nerve injury in her tail after incidents of having it stepped on in the dark or boxes falling on it, leading to bouts of furiously attacking her tail. It was after months of neglectful treatment that she and I crossed paths, igniting in my heart a love as vast as the ocean. Instantly, I knew I was her forever 'hooman' and that, beyond Princess's scars, a great potential for courage and recovery within her fragile frame was apparent.

Our bond formed steadily, built upon patience, understanding, and unwavering devotion. My touch became a source of comfort for Princess, a beacon of hope in the darkness that had once consumed her. In my arms, Princess found solace, a sanctuary where the wounds of the past could begin to heal. It was a privilege to feel her trust and love grow with each passing day!

As Princess navigated the trials and tribulations of her own journey, she did so with the knowledge that she was not alone. In my household, each of our previous animal companions was given royal names because of their regal dispositions and presence. In the whispers of the wind and the rustle of the leaves, it was clear that she heard the voices of her lineage, guiding her with their timeless wisdom and unwavering love—a testament to the enduring power of love. Among her esteemed lineage were her royal feline siblings: Queen LaLa, with her piercing emerald eyes, and Kingy Shah, with his dignified bearing, who shared a pillar of strength and devotion for Princess. Also part of this esteemed lineage was Princess's favorite: her uncle, King Archie, though canine, whose imperial stature and gentle demeanor embodied the essence of nobility, his presence a beacon of inspiration for all who crossed his path.

Yet, Princess's journey was far from easy. As days turned into weeks and weeks into months, it became evident that Princess's past had left a lasting mark on her fragile body. Though the nerves in her tail had physically recovered, Princess continued to recall the pain in her body upon introduction of any fear, stress, or loud noise, and the attacks on her tail persisted with regular frequency and intensity. It was the nervous system impairment that plagued her, threatening to steal away the precious moments of joy that she had found in my company.

In the face of adversity, I resolved to remain steadfast by Princess's side. Together, we navigated the complexities of veterinary appointments, medication regimens, and moments of uncertainty and anguish. Through it all, our bond only grew stronger, a testament to the resilience of love in the face of hardship. Though her body may have been weakened by neglect, trauma, and injury, her spirit remained unbroken. Princess opened her heart to love and found the strength to persevere, fighting against the darkness that threatened to consume her. In caring for Princess, I discovered a newfound sense of purpose and resilience within myself. Our shared journey became a profound source of inspiration, reminding me of the extraordinary lengths that love can propel us toward.

As Princess's journey unfolded, we explored various avenues of traditional and holistic healing. Collaborating closely with veterinary providers, healers, and behaviorists, our goal was to bridge the gap between Princess's world and ours so that she could find relief. Through this multi-disciplinary approach, we gained deeper insights into her well-being and nurtured our bond of trust and understanding.

Specialty veterinarians, which included veterinary neurologists, proved to be invaluable allies in Princess's battle against illness. With their expertise and guidance, we navigated the complexities of her condition, finding comfort in knowing that Princess was in the hands of skilled professionals dedicated to her well-being. Additionally, holistic veterinarians played a pivotal role in Princess's care, adopting a comprehensive approach that encompassed her physical, emotional, and spiritual well-being. Together, we embarked on a healing journey that honored Princess's unique needs and celebrated her brave and loving spirit.

Yet, her trauma continued to manifest in response to stressors, causing attacks on her tail and confounding her multi-disciplinary veterinary team. Princess remained a steadfast and loving partner, collaborating tirelessly with each practitioner and placing her trust in our love and care. Though she sometimes clearly signaled her limits, our loving relationship encouraged her to embrace new experiences and opportunities for healing. Seeking out my own support helped me attune myself to Princess's needs, ensuring that I comprehended her physical, emotional, and social requirements at every stage. Our connection grew stronger as we faced challenges and celebrated triumphs together on Princess's healing journey, bound by our unwavering commitment.

We persisted in pursuit of recovery. Animal behaviorists provided invaluable insights into Princess's behavior, helping us address challenges. With their guidance, we gained a deeper understanding of Princess's unique personality and learned to communicate with her in a way that honored her individuality and respected her boundaries. Energy healers provided yet another dimension of healing for Princess, tapping into the subtle energies that flow through all living beings. With their gentle care and profound understanding of energy medicine, they helped restore balance and harmony within Princess's body and spirit. Through the incorporation of these gentle approaches, Princess began to release the trauma stored in her body, and her tail found relief from the attacks as her nervous system settled. Her healing lay in the safety and security of love.

Witnessing her journey inspired me to honor my own need for security and peace. As Princess's healing journey progressed, a new chapter awaited us on the horizon—a journey from New England to the Sunshine State. The decision to relocate was not made lightly, but I knew that the warmer climate and tropical surroundings held the promise of new beginnings and healing for Princess. I was terrified that the stress of the travel would wreak havoc on her tail attacks. Of course, consulting with her team of traditional and holistic veterinary providers and energetic healers allowed for support through the transport at every step of the way.

The journey began with places unknown to Princess as we made our way southward toward our destination. Three continuous days of car travel tested both of our endurance, but Princess remained steadfast by my heart, her unwavering presence a source of comfort and reassurance. Her energetic healing team supported us by helping to calm both Princess and me, allowing me to provide reassurance and comfort when Princess felt agitated. This warded off attacks on her tail during our days of continuous driving.

At the airport, we encountered a mishap that threatened to derail our plans and led to a lengthy day awaiting the last rung of our travel, but Princess's indomitable spirit and determination saw us through. Her team of support assuaged her distress and relieved her agitation. She was a model of mindfulness and presence! Boarding the plane, we embarked on the final leg of our journey, the anticipation of our destination lifting our weariness.

As the plane descended toward the Sunshine State, Princess and I, both wide-eyed and curious, looked forward to the replenishment of our new surroundings. Upon landing, we stepped out into the fresh air of our new home and were greeted by loving friends who had anxiously awaited Princess's arrival well into the late hours of the night.

In that moment, as Princess basked in the warmth of the tropical climate, surrounded by the love and support of her newfound family, I promised her the sun, too, would greet her in the morning. We knew that her healing journey, while not yet over, was coming to a close. I felt so proud of her courage and bravery throughout the voyage! With each step forward, guided by love and fueled by determination, Princess embraced the challenges and adventures ahead of her, her spirit shining bright like the sun that now bathes her in its golden light.

With each passing day, she shines brighter, her spirit illuminated by the light of her heart and spirit. As she continues on her journey, Princess carries with her the legacy of those who came before her, a legacy of love, resilience, and unyielding grace. More importantly, Princess steps forth with her own legacy of courage to remain open to not only giving love but also receiving love. Though not formally an ESA, she adeptly brightens the day for those she encounters with emotional support and elevates oxytocin with affectionate snuggles.

Under the right conditions, love, safety, trust, joy, and magic flourish. Princess allowed love to transform the fear and pain from her early trauma into the healing light of love and courage, shedding the limitations of her past and embracing a life immersed in joy. Today, Princess's tale of healing stands as a beacon of hope and inspiration for all who hear it. Despite beginning in darkness, her journey is defined by the light she embraced. Through unwavering love and resilience, she turned pain into healing, fear into courage, and despair into a new beginning in life. Her journey vividly illustrates how animals inspire us to navigate emotional struggles and traumas.

Bio

Dr. Nazari is a clinical psychologist, certified spiritual advisor, animal communicator, registered yoga instructor, and certified meditation teacher. She offers psychospiritual healing to people and animals through a unique blend of holistic and psychological services.

Dr. Nazari is passionate about living a fulfilled life in

harmony with what brings us joy and aligns with our higher purpose. She is a best-selling author and regular contributor to publications, as well as host of her podcast, Beyond the Couch with Dr. Sally. Her goal is to help people and animals spiritually and emotionally connect with their higher selves to live a life they celebrate every day.

WEBSITE: www.drsallynazari.com
EMAIL: drnazari@drsallynazari.com

"When we accept we are all connected by something greater than ourselves, even if inexplicable, we know love is what binds us, and with love, we can heal."

Rosanne Groover Norris

Chapter Thirteen
Ruby Returns
By Rosanne Groover Norris

I had no intention of getting a dog, but Fritz was a gift that would not be denied.

In meditation on a cold January morning in 2020, a dog popped into my awareness. It flashed in and out of my mind's eye, but I was sure it looked like a Schnauzer. Strange. Why would I see a Schnauzer? I never owned one or knew anyone who did. I had never had a vision like this, so I was surprised by this experience. I questioned whether I saw it at all.

When I explained what had happened to my husband, he said he had been researching dogs the day before, thinking he might surprise me with a puppy for my birthday, which was not until June. He said he was intrigued by the Miniature Schnauzer.

How interesting.

I marveled at this connection but wasn't all that surprised. I had read how our brains act as antennas, sending and receiving consciousness and sharing information.

That I had maybe tapped into my husband's stream of consciousness made sense to me. But why had we shared this information? There must be a reason.

We discussed the idea of having a dog and dismissed it as not the right time.

Then I got curious.

We traveled to visit family that day, so I decided to research Miniature Schnauzers. A local breeder's website came up with six or seven puppies available. Puppies are cute. It can't hurt to look, right?

As I scrolled through the faces of those cute puppies, I was drawn to one little pup. The photo was less clear than the others, but for some reason, I kept going back to look at that blurry photo. It wasn't until the third or fourth look I realized it was available on the exact day my son had passed two years prior.

I was stunned. How could this be? Was this a coincidence? Or something more?

The Oxford Dictionary defines a coincidence as "a remarkable concurrence of events or circumstances without apparent causal connection." Merriam-Webster defines a coincidence as "the occurrence of events that happen at the same time by accident but seem to have a connection."

I felt there was a connection.

In the late 20s or early 30s, Psychologist Carl Jung introduced the idea of synchronicity, in which two unrelated events or circumstances seem to have a connection. From this description, it seems Jung and Webster are saying the same thing. Science explains these events in terms of probability rather than connection. For example, according to an article written by Robert Matthew for sciencefocus.com, there is "almost a 50:50 chance of at least two of the 23 players in any football match having the same birthday." Okay, this makes sense to me. Probability is how likely something happens. It's in the numbers.

However, I was not even looking for a dog, so I am not sure probability applies.

Jung believed the events that happen to us can hold a special meaning even though one thing did not cause the other to happen. I'm with Jung.

But back to Fritz's story.

I made a call to the breeder to arrange a visit for the next day. We arrived to find two litters of puppies squirming inside a corral in the breeder's living room. She pointed out the puppy, a three-pound runt among his boisterous peers. She said he had personality, and watching him, it was clear he was not intimidated by the others. I held him, unsure I wanted the responsibility of owning a dog. It had been nine years since we said goodbye to Ruby, our family beagle. I thanked the breeder and told her we would think about this monumental decision.

On the way home, we discussed the pros and cons of having a dog. We agreed it would be a game-changer. Every decision, from going out to dinner to going on vacation, would have to factor in a dog. Call it a coincidence or synchronicity, I couldn't shake the feeling he was meant to be ours, and quite possibly a gift from our son. And that was that. I called the breeder, and a few days later, we brought him home.

When this little three-pound runt walked into the house, he sat down, sniffed, and looked around like he knew the place. I had set up a bed inside a little corral like he was used to with his roommates. I was prepared for the sleepless nights I was sure would happen like it does with most new puppies, but what did happen surprised me. He slept contentedly from the very first night.

Miniature Schnauzers are originally from Germany, but that is not why he bears the name. I was told by a medium I would write a book about my son's death, assisted by a German guide with a long name beginning with an F, which I would shorten. I started hearing the word "book" several times a day. I felt like I was being pestered by something or someone. I knew I would write the book, but I was reluctant to start it, knowing it would be a difficult task. Then, one night, I woke to strong German words in my head. Now, I don't speak or understand German, but I did comprehend the tone of the voice telling me it was time to start the book. When I silently asked what I should call him, I heard the name "Fritz." I wrote the book and never heard German words again, but I honored my writing guide by naming my dog after him.

Spunky, sweet Fritz had us wrapped around his paw right from the beginning. He was smart and easy to house train, unlike our beagle, Ruby, who we had to send over the Rainbow Bridge in 2011. Ruby was a sweet dog but quite stubborn, as beagles are known to be, and not nearly as bright as this new little pup seemed to be. But we loved her all the same.

A few weeks after Fritz came into our lives, I recalled a strange experience I had months before that now had me curious. One night, as I was falling asleep, I felt a depression behind me on the bed. I was puzzled and thought my husband was getting in on the wrong side. Then I felt something walking around the bed, like an animal would. It was dark in the room, so I felt where my husband normally slept without opening my eyes, but he wasn't there. As the walking continued, a thought came to me. Ruby? I immediately felt tingles all over, along with a burst of love. I had never had an experience like this, and I wasn't sure what to make of it. As I drifted off to sleep, I sent gratitude to Ruby and Lee, thinking perhaps this was a sign that they are together.

I now know it was more.

Reincarnation wasn't a concept I grew up with, but I was familiar with it now. I had read stories about very young children who knew things they couldn't have known about the lives they had lived in the past, and when researched, they turned out to be accurate. It didn't dawn on me that a pet might be able to do the same until I researched it. Later, a medium confirmed Fritz was indeed a reincarnation of Ruby, who wanted to come back to help me heal. What a selfless act of love. There is no way I can prove this, but it rings true in my heart.

It doesn't matter what you call these experiences. When we understand we are all connected by something greater than ourselves, even if inexplicable, we know love is what binds us, and with love, we can heal. Fritz and I have a connection beyond that of pet and owner. When I look at Fritz, I feel the love of Lee and Ruby pouring through his eyes. And that is a gift for which I am forever grateful.

Bio

Rosanne Norris embarked on a spiritual path in 2018 after her thirty-year-old son, Lee, passed unexpectedly. She is an affiliate leader and caring listener for Helping Parents Heal, an organization that helps parents after the loss of a child.

Rosanne is an author of beLEEve: a Journey of Loss, Healing, and Hope (2020) and a contributor to four anthologies: Ordinary Oneness: The Simplicity of Everyday Love, Grace and Hope (2021), Gathering at the Doorway: An Anthology of Signs, Visits, and Messages from the Afterlife (2022), Ignite Your Inner Fire (2023), and Awaken Your Magic (2024).

Rosanne was also featured in the award-winning documentary Rinaldi, the story of Brazilian transcommunication researcher Sonia Rinaldi. For over thirty years, she has brought through images and voices from deceased loved ones.

Additionally, Rosanne is a Reiki Master and a certified grief educator, trained by the world-renowned David Kessler.

She can be reached at rmnorris457@gmail.com

Chapter Fourteen
27 Dogs
By Natasha Pecarski

I've been blessed to be surrounded by dogs my entire life, but this story of healing and transformation is thanks to other people's dogs, 27 of them to be exact. For you to understand how they've helped me on my journey and how they came into my life, I need to take you back to where it all started, that moment when I needed these dogs the most.

I believed I could do it all. Plus, I was guilty of not setting boundaries and struggled with a lack of confidence and belief in myself. I lived in the future, loved with conditions, ignored my intuition, lacked consistency, and took life way too seriously. In addition to these detrimental behaviors, I accepted demanding career opportunities and encountered some personal hurdles in my life. Sprinkle a little pandemic into the mix, and I hit rock bottom in October 2021.

What I thought would be a 3-week vacation from work led to a 7-month leave. Little did I know that I was suffering from an intense burnout. Like most people in my situation, I turned inward and created a cocoon for myself. I stopped talking to my friends and family to quiet all the noise and evaluate where things had gone wrong.

The first thing I realized was that I needed a better work-life balance. My kids are growing up fast, and I felt like I was missing crucial moments in their lives. I thought that perhaps having a dog in our home was what I needed. What better way to recover from burnout than with a dog's unconditional love and attention? There's a reason why dogs are brought to visit patients in hospitals and aging adults in retirement homes. They support a person's mental health by providing them comfort. I believed they could do the same for me.

Midway through my leave, I knew my employer would start asking about my return to work, but I knew I wasn't ready. I felt like I was still living in my cocoon and had a lot more work ahead of me. The last thing I wanted to do was to fall back into old patterns and find myself back at square one. This forced me to take matters into my own hands and I began exploring other career options. This is when I thought of a colleague who had established a side income by welcoming dogs into his home when their owners were away. I contacted the company he worked for so I could do the same. Oddly enough, several weeks went by and they never replied. That silence pushed me onto a path I never anticipated.

After several months of research, training, and certification, I opened my first-ever small business, Happy House Guest, and started to welcome fur babies into my home. Even though it was terrifying to go out on my own, everything fell into place seamlessly—proof that the universe was directing me to the exact thing I needed to do for myself and my family.

This brings us to the present day. After two years of being in business, I've had the pleasure of meeting 27 dogs. Some encounters have been brief, while others have been in my care for a while, and I can't forget the ones who've crossed the rainbow bridge. Even though they weren't my dogs, their passing impacted my life immensely, and to this day, I still miss the love and laughter they brought into my house and my heart. Despite the length of time, every single one of my guests has had a profound impact on my life, not only in terms of emotional support but also in teaching me valuable life lessons so I could recover from a temporary burnout and start living my life to its fullest.

7 Lessons from 27 Dogs

(1) Dogs thrive when they have boundaries, and I discovered that I needed to do the same. I've set

boundaries—as a business owner and in my personal life—and this allows me to focus on what matters most.

(2) Dogs can feel their leader's energy transmitted through the leash while walking, as well as in their body language and voice. I had no other choice but to exude more confidence and demonstrate that I believe in myself and my skills. This proved to be extremely successful while training them, and it has helped me tremendously in other aspects of my life.

(3) Dogs explore the world through their sense of smell; therefore, I take my house guests on sniff-aris. This allows them to sniff whatever they want and leads me wherever they want to go. During these thousands of walks, I learned the importance of being fully present and enjoying the moment. As a result, I feel like I'm no longer missing crucial moments in my life and now appreciate the small things life offers.

(4) Dogs live and breathe unconditional love, which reminded me that this is the only way to love. Every dog in my care is always there for me through thick and thin while lending a listening ear without judgment. Because of this, I learned to offer love freely, expect nothing in return, and listen without judgment.

(5) Dogs are known to trust their intuition, and they taught

me to trust mine. Whenever I face an unfamiliar situation or something challenging, I now follow my gut feeling, and it's never led me astray. It leads me to my next step or my next lesson.

(6) Dogs need consistency to prevent behavioral issues but, most importantly, to boost their canine confidence. I was reminded that I need to be more consistent in my life so I can reach my goals and make positive, lasting changes. It's not about perfection. It's about progress.

(7) Dogs are always ready to play. They remind me every day of its importance. I no longer take life too seriously. Now, I embrace playfulness and always make time to have fun, laugh, and be silly. Laughter is, indeed, the best medicine.

These 27 dogs have not only helped me but my children as well. They've learned that different breeds have different characteristics and that each dog has its unique personality and needs. As a result, they've learned to be flexible and adapt their approach to each dog that is in our care. I've seen them become more confident, and assume the role of pack leader when they help walk or train them. These are amazing life lessons to learn at such a young age.

Overall, the whole experience has brought my family

closer together. We work as a team, and we all have our part to play when we meet new clients and when their fur baby is in our home. Opening Happy House Guest has even inspired my kids to potentially become small business owners one day. I'm extremely proud that I've been able to show them that hard work, taking calculated risks, and having the courage to follow your dreams can pay off in more ways than one.

My decision to open this business not only provided me with the work-life balance I wanted and needed, but it also became a platform for my personal growth. I'm a different person from my pre-burnout self. Through my experience with these dogs, I've learned the importance of setting boundaries, exuding confidence, being more present, offering unconditional love, trusting my intuition, striving for consistency, and embracing playfulness in life. All of which has transformed me into a more confident, balanced, and fulfilled woman.

To those families that have trusted me with these 27 dogs, thank you. I'm forever changed.

If you know your angel numbers, 7 and 27 means: (7) *"You're on the right path. Keep up the good work"* and (27) *"Continue on your path with faith. You're doing the right thing, so keep up the good work". (Angel Number by Doreen Virtue and Lynette Brown)*

Note to the universe: I hear you loud and clear, and I'll continue on this path.

Bio

Natasha Pecarski is the owner of Happy House Guest, where she and her family board dogs in their home. She's a proud mother of two amazing kids and a wife to her loving and supportive husband. Natasha's a project manager of all things, and a leader in health and wellness with the goal of changing lives, one person at a time. As a trained dancer, she never shies away from a great kitchen dance party.

This is her first published story. Despite it being difficult for her to step out of her comfort zone, she wanted to share her story to inspire others to face their fears, pursue their dreams, and prioritize their happiness. She hopes her journey will serve as a reminder that even in our darkest moments, there's always the potential for healing, growth, and transformation. She can be reached at happyhouseguestottawa@gmail.com.

Chapter Fifteen
Fluffy Furry Fairy
By Sylvie Robert

It was love at first sight! I had been looking for her for such a long time. This loving, energetic, fun female 4-pound Yorkshire Terrier stole my heart the moment our eyes locked in! She was a young adult, frail, nervous and scared in her cage, but when I held her in my arms for the first time, she started kissing me all over my face. She was so excited, I almost dropped her! Then she calmed down and rested her head on my shoulder, locking it near my neck as if to say: "I found you. I am home now." I knew she was the one. My search was over! A one-of-a-kind, never-ending unconditional love story started that day. I decided to name her Toutsie, which in French slang means "toute petite," and in English, it means "really small."

From Abuse to Freedom

She was too tiny to have puppies, so they decided to sell her. I thought I had saved her as she was trembling, sad, agitated, anxious, and scared at the store. But it was the other way around. She was my magical fairy, my protective angel, who would stand by me through thick and thin. She was a bundle of joy! Little did I know she would be my rock, my biggest support through it all!

I had started a long-term relationship. I eventually got married out of love, but it became an abusive relationship over time. I truly loved him and wanted to make our marriage a success, but it takes two to accomplish this. I made the bold decision to end this book, bringing it to a close in my life. I am grateful and now free to be myself. What a relief to be able to laugh when you feel like it!

I remember falling asleep at night out of exhaustion after crying too much, mostly in my pillow. That way, he wouldn't hear me bawling. I knew a trick to keep a spoon in the freezer. I could then put it on my eyes in the morning to remove the puffiness to be able to go to work. My sweet dog Toutsie was always coming to console me, to comfort me and to give me love. She would sleep tucked in while cuddling in between my knees. She would moan if I changed positions at night, but I knew how to change without moving her. She was spoiled, too! I loved her so much! She knew exactly how I felt anytime!

With her unwavering support, I was able to navigate the tumultuous waters of my separation, divorce and annulment as the abuse was proven on his part. Her support and love were invaluable in helping me come out the other side stronger and more resilient. I wouldn't change a thing because my past experiences have shaped me into the person I am today. It also propelled me to take healing courses to heal myself and develop my skills. Toutsie was undoubtedly a gift from heaven, supporting me and loving me every step of the way. Holding this furry, loving, joyful 4-pound dog made my heart smile! I am deeply grateful!

Facing Adversity with Fearlessness

Coming back from my parents' place in Moonbeam in January 2007, I brought back my faithful companion Toutsie home. She was at my parents' place while I went to take one of my certification classes with Deepak Chopra at the Chopra Centre in California.

When I came back, much to my dismay, I saw she had a big cyst on her throat. I immediately contacted the veterinarian to get some advice and an appointment at their earliest convenience. We were leaving the following day to go back to Ottawa. After driving ten hours back home and being sick myself, too, I went to bed right away as she had an appointment at the clinic first thing in the morning.

In the middle of the night, I was awakened by a constant loud sound of licking. I still remember vividly that night!

I turned around and saw my dear Toutsie on the floor licking herself as she had taken her cyst out and was licking herself to keep herself clean. She seemed calm. I jumped out of bed and immediately did some healing and called in the fairies, as they are the guardian angels of animals. I took the hydrogen peroxide to clean her so no infection would come out of this. I stayed up with her even though I wasn't well myself. She is my world, my love, and I would have done anything for her to be well, happy and healthy!

In the early hours, I brought her to the specialist. As a toy Yorkie, the operation to remove her cyst at that location would have been dangerous, and her chances to live were slim to none. She had the smallest throat. By removing it herself, she saved herself! I was in awe! Toutsie healed herself safely! What an Amazing dog!

Familiarizing Ourselves with the Spirit World

Every time someone new entered my home, my faithful protective dog would bark and growl to let them know that it was her home. She was protecting me from strangers, either living or in spirit. She also welcomed the ones she knew well with kisses and a happy dance!

After I had learned to help deceased loved ones cross into the light in my shamanic classes, lots of spirits came to me for help. Toutsie was barking a lot as they were strangers to both of us and would appear out of nowhere. They would surprise her at night in the bedroom. It made her stressed and anxious. I loved helping another spirit cross into the light; it couldn't be at Toutsie's expense. I had to find a way to help her!

I decided to use some animal communication tools I had learned for the first time. To connect my heart chakra to her heart chakra, my throat chakra to her throat chakra and my third eye chakra to her third eye chakra and then to talk to her. I had nothing to lose and everything to gain. Why not!

I connected the chakras energetically and started to explain to Toutsie that spirits were only coming to get help to cross into the light. I remember seeing one, and it took me by surprise! Back then, I preferred to only feel them. Toutsie could see them for me and let me know where they were. She only needed to bark twice and then show me the direction. Then, I would take care of them. She had nothing else to do. I didn't know if it would work, but I wanted her to be calm and happy and not stressed or anxious.

That same night, Toutsie barked twice, so I asked her the location of the spirit needing help, and she turned her head and faced my bathroom door. Her tail was wagging, and she was panting. It seemed like she was smiling happily, being proud of herself! Wow! I was ecstatic! Communication with animals does work! I thanked her, and she lay her head calmly on her paws. She let me help the spirits without stressing herself.

I realized later that there was a portal in my bathroom attached to my bedroom. This explained why all the new spirits came into my bedroom; it was through that portal. I love helping them cross into the light, but I needed to sleep at night; therefore I closed the portal energetically and decided that no spirit would wake me up at night unless it was an emergency. They can come to my healing sessions during the daytime. We are the ones who determine our boundaries. Choose wisely. You must help yourself first to be able to help even more people. Self-care is of utmost importance.

Favorable Outcome

I decided to take a nap in the afternoon. I was on the verge of falling asleep when I heard my dog bark twice and simultaneously felt the energy and the air around me getting colder. I turned around and saw my dog facing my computer desk. I knew a spirit was in the room. I was so tired and said: "If it is an emergency, send me another sign; otherwise, I need to have a nap right now." I knew the portal was closed. My clairsentience was stronger than my clairvoyance at that moment, which is the reason I asked for another sign to validate the urgency.

I noticed that my computer's light had turned on, and I could hear my printer starting to print something. My computer and printer were both off before! I got up right away. I knew it was a deceased loved one asking for some urgent help on behalf of someone else, but I didn't know whom. To help, I needed to know who required assistance, so I asked the spirit to send me another sign. The printer started to print again. I decided to check my emails. I then saw an email from a family member asking for help for a loved one who was in critical condition at the hospital, and they didn't know if the loved one would survive the operation. She was in intensive care and was going for an emergency heart surgery, with her chance of survival being slim to none! The spirit who came to get my help had died a couple of days earlier. I was surprised she was able to come and get my attention. I knew it took everything for that spirit to contact me. She had to be determined for sure! She had said hurtful words to the loved one right before she died and therefore came to amend by getting me involved to help the loved one.

I got up right away. After getting permission from the loved one's higher self, I started to do some distant healing. It was one of my first distant healing sessions. It was an emergency, and I had to step up to help as it was crucial; *every minute counted*. I did the healing for one hour and then fell asleep on the couch for two hours. I was then woken up by a phone call from another family member telling me that the doctors didn't understand how everything changed rapidly and that much! The operation was a total success! Her heart was well again! Thanks to the deceased loved one and my sidekick Toutsie for getting my attention. My Yorkie remained calm the whole time my deceased loved one was present. Together, we can create miracles!

Fly Me to Heaven

The last time I saw Toutsie alive, we both knew it was the last time, even if I was supposed to see her in a couple of weeks. There were major constructions in my apartment building, and they were changing all the patios and elevators. The sound was unbearable for my poor Yorkie, so the plan was to keep her at my parents' place until the construction was over. I also knew she was in good hands with them. Toutsie also loved them all!

I will always remember that she didn't want me to leave that day. My heart was breaking. I had to leave, as it was already late in the afternoon. I knew I would arrive late at night and work the next morning. She looked at me with her head tilted to the side to better understand me, her eyes filled with love. as if she knew it was the last time. I had tears rolling down my cheeks. We both knew. I gave her a big hug and kisses. I told her how much I loved her and how much she made a big difference in my life. Sometimes, we must make sacrifices for the benefit of our loved ones. Her well-being was more important to me. She passed away peacefully in her sleep next to her beloved canine companion a couple of days later! She was surrounded by unconditional love.

I was missing her dearly. I remember vividly the time she came to visit me in spirit. I was lying in bed reminiscing our time together, and then I felt footsteps on the mattress. I felt the mattress sink the same way when she used to climb the stairs and come to bed. Then I felt her presence between my knees, where she would come to sleep with me all the time. I didn't dare to move. I was happy she came to bring me some love. It was needed. She also came often in my dreams when I needed her. It was a lucid dream where I would see her happy, barking and panting as she wanted to show me that she had done it in the litter again. She knew she would get a treat after. Other times, I saw her in my dream running around, no more aging pain, full of energy, joy and love. She was well, and she wanted me to know she was at peace and still wanted to be around me.

As I was writing her story in her honor, she came again to visit me. This time, she was with my current Siberian cat named Belle. Toutsie came to greet me, give me some love and share her happiness. I then saw her shapeshift into a young lady in her mid-twenties, and she ran into my arms to hug me. Belle, my cat, morphed into a younger female child and hugged me. I always wanted to have children, and now I had my two girls in my arms! What a gift bestowed upon me! Thank you, universe!

Bio

Sylvie Robert is a Shaman, an Amazing Healer, an International Spiritual Teacher, a Singing Medium and a Spirited Speaker. Her divine mission is to shine her pure white light and help others shine their pure white light!

Sylvie is a Master Reiki and a Master Instructor of Integrated Energy Therapy@Healing with the Angels. She's a Chopra Center Certified Instructor to teach Primordial Sound Meditation with Deepak Chopra, an Akashic Record Consultant from the Akashic Knowing School of Wisdom and a Certified Teacher with The Four Winds Society to teach Dying Consciously. Sylvie has completed Shamanic Energy Medicine and Munay-ki with Alberto Villoldo. She teaches the Cosmic Rites.

Sylvie is also a Certified Angel Card Reader and Angel

Numerologist with Radleigh Valentine. Sylvie completed The Journey Practitioner with Brandon Bays. She studied Intermediate and Advanced Mediumship with Tim Abbot at the Arthur Findlay Spiritualist College in England. She also studied with John Holland, Sharon Anne Klingler, Janet Nohavec and Lisa Williams. Sylvie furthered her skills with the Shamans in Peru and studied with Neale Donald Walsch and Sonia Choquette. She's a Clutter and Clearing Coach with Denise Linn. Sylvie has been seen for years on Rogers TV on Nat en Parle! www.facebook.com/munaysonko

Chapter Sixteen
Essence Over Form
By Kyra Schaefer

We never would have intentionally chosen a pitbull, yet we wouldn't have excluded one either – a pitty was simply not on our radar.

But let me take a step back.

After losing our cherished Logan, a black Labrador Retriever that Todd raised from a puppy, the thought of opening ourselves up to potential heartbreak again seemed nearly impossible. After nine months of waiting, the weight became unbearable for me. I sought solace at the Animal Welfare League in Phoenix, hoping a furry friend might call out to me. I asked the staff to show me dogs suitable for our hypnotherapy clinic, ones comfortable around people. Despite my efforts, I couldn't find that connection. As we were leaving, my gaze landed behind the front desk, revealing a white, curly-tailed 25 lb Spitz Mix. "What about him?" I asked. "Oh, yes," they replied, "recently returned by a pregnant woman who found caring for him too challenging." My instincts kicked in, and he was undeniably a cutie. I watched him at the dog park, sassy yet not overwhelming, just eager to be part of the action. I fell in love. While there was a two-day 'sleepover' policy at the time, anyone who knows me knows once an animal enters my house, they don't leave!

With Jack comfortably settled into the Schaefer household, Todd felt the yearning for another canine companion. Setting an intention and focusing on essence over form, he clarified the desired personality of our next dog. He would think about her personality daily, and often, he would talk about her as if she were there with us already. Multiple trips to different pounds yielded no energetic match. Despite attempts to introduce Jack to potential dogs, no resonance was found. In fact, many dogs we tried to match him with became violent in his presence.

Until one day.

Jack accompanied us on our quest to find the perfect match. Todd had already named our yet-to-be-met dog Honey, often mentioning she was "coming home soon."

On this particular day, as I walked ahead, I noticed Todd wasn't close behind. Turning around, I saw the cutest scene unfold.

Todd was reaching his fingers through the tight mesh fencing of a pin, and a 60-lb pitbull had flattened herself against the fence, eager to get as close to him as possible. It was pure essence. This brindle, black-masked, drop-eared pitbull exuded strength and warmth, unexpected in form but absolutely spot on in essence. She recently had puppies, adding complexity to her story as she was rescued from a puppy mill.

Honey's meeting with Jack was uneventful. It felt like they had known each other forever. He was completely at ease around her, and she was at ease around him. I was shocked, considering all the other dogs' reactions to him were so uncomfortable.

We brought her home for a 'spend the night,' knowing well that she was the *one*. She began to settle into our family but there were some issues in the beginning. Clearly traumatized in various ways, she displayed unique reactions, particularly to nail trimming and the sound of young puppies. Yet, as a family, we were confident we could help her heal.

What unfolded next was surprising.

Once trained, Honey transformed into our in-clinic therapy dog. Todd worked with her day and night, along with a trainer, to help her become a Good Samaritan Therapy Dog. She would gracefully lie with our clients during both group and individual sessions, becoming a requested presence for those on their healing journey.

Certainly, sacrifices were made along the way. The sheer cost of caring for a dog limited our travels. Pitbull discrimination prevented us from moving to other rental homes. And, the unruly nature of other dogs kept Honey away from dog parks, as her protective instincts could lead to unwarranted blame. But, I wouldn't trade her for anything. She is precious to us, a cherished family member and companion—the sweetest Honey Bee in the whole world. Manifested through profound feelings of unconditional love, Todd found the perfect energetic match in Honey, and as a family, we never let go.

When it comes to manifesting anything, it's vital to let go of the form you seek. Allow the feeling you want to experience to permeate all thoughts. Practice that good feeling daily. Speak about what you are creating as if it were already with you, and the essence will call to you when you come near it. Whether it's a beloved pet, a beautiful home, or a new career, letting go of the form will surpass expectations 10,000-fold.

Bio

Kyra Schaefer, Co-Founder and CEO of As You Wish Publishing, a venture established with her husband, Todd Schaefer, has dedicated the past seven years to empowering individuals to illuminate their unique essence and share their narratives with the world. Leading As You Wish Publishing, Kyra spearheads the publication of collaborative and solo books, available in print and ebook formats.

The diverse array of books produced by As You Wish Publishing, whether authored individually or through collaboration, cover a broad spectrum of topics such as self-discovery, personal journeys, healing, holistic business, therapeutic modalities, coaching, and spirituality. Kyra, alongside her husband, has successfully collaborated with numerous authors, embracing a variety of ages, writing styles, and creative approaches.

Beyond her role as a bestselling and award-winning author renowned for "Holograms and Echoes: Transform Triggers to Truth," Kyra Schaefer's passion extends to creating empowering, joyful, and insightful workshops tailored for small groups. Her expertise also spans certifications in Positive Psychology, Art Therapy, and as a Master Practitioner in Neurolinguistics and Hypnosis. With a rich career spanning two decades, Kyra has positively impacted thousands of clients in her role as an emotional therapy practitioner.

Reach Kyra at connect@asyouwishpublishing.com or via the web at www.asyouwishpublishing.com

Chapter Seventeen

Lessons From An Enchanted Peanut

By YuSon Shin

In the timeless annals of fairy tales, one often hears of Jack and his five enchanted beans, which sprouted into a towering beanstalk leading to the realm of giants. But for me, the magic lay in an unexpected form—a single, enchanted peanut who taught me to slay my giant fears and limitations and revealed to me a world of wisdom and magic. Allow me to introduce Princess Peanut Mini Muffin: my beautiful twelve-and-a-half-pound, black and tan Chihuahua mix. Much like Yoda from *Star Wars*, she was my pint-sized guru.

Fate brought us together when I was forty years old. At that time, I felt like a Padawan searching for a Jedi teacher like Yoda to show me the way. I had so many questions without answers. I was in a place of limbo, a place of in-between. My life was neither good nor bad. I was neither young nor old. I was still triggered by childhood trauma but old enough to handle things better than I was. I was raised by fearful parents, plus my father was abusive. I can hear Peanut channeling Yoda's gravelly voice, saying, "Fear is the path to the dark side. Fear leads to anger. Anger leads to hate. Hate leads to suffering." Because I was in a place of neither here nor there, many describe this state as "lost" or "stuck," and I was suffering. With almost fifteen years of healing studies under my belt, I often contemplated doing it full-time, but the courage to let go of my steady paycheck from my job as a paralegal eluded me. Yoda would say, "Your path you must decide." Peanut would add, "Enjoy the walk." Inspired by these wise sentiments, I took the next steps toward my calling.

Peanut was magic in an unassuming package. She even knew how to make an entrance by sending me a sign that she was coming. About six months before she arrived, I got a weird mammogram result on my left breast, which led to the extra step of an ultrasound. The ultrasound technician showed me the image and said, "See. It looks like a peanut over your heart." All tests were normal afterward.

Before Peanut's arrival, I asked the universe almost daily for a great spiritual teacher. I was not ready for my teacher to be a dog. Despite a myriad of obstacles—an apartment complex that banned pets, my allergies, and my inexperience with dogs—Peanut found her way into my life. I say that I rescued her, but she rescued me.

I was having lunch with a friend, and we decided to walk off our lunch at an indoor mall called the Beverly Center. A woman was walking around with a sleeping puppy the size of the palm of her hand, trying to sell her as a teacup Chihuahua for $500. She was encouraging everyone to hold Chanel, Peanut's previous moniker, in hopes that she would make a sale. In conversation, she mentioned that she was on welfare and couldn't afford veterinary care, so she gave Chanel and all her littermates whole cloves of garlic to de-worm them. Even though I had no dog experience, I knew that garlic was toxic for dogs. Without thinking, I went into rescue mode, made an offer of $100, and took her home, where I was going to meet my best friend, Brian. When Brian met my new fur baby, he started talking to her in a high-pitched voice and calling her a little peanut. The minute I heard him say it, I knew it was her name. It wasn't until months after adopting her I remembered what the ultrasound technician said about the peanut-shaped image near my heart. Peanut had to come in the guise of rescue because I don't think I would have adopted a dog otherwise.

Like other people who have experienced childhood toxic stress, I like the comfort and safety of routine. The dog adoption threw a wrench into my usual routine, so my brain tried to create a new routine incorporating Peanut. On our walks, I took her on the same route for about a month with only two goals in mind: exercising and doing her business. One day, she firmly slammed on the brakes as dogs do. She looked up at me, and I knew she was saying, "No!" Peanut, with her insatiable curiosity, challenged my penchant for predictability. Afterward, each walk became an adventure, an opportunity to view the world through her eyes and nose and embrace spontaneity. She reminded me that growth lay beyond the confines of routine, urging me to embrace life's unpredictability.

Peanut came to heal and serve as a catalyst for change. Since my instinct was to prioritize others over myself, Peanut used herself to motivate me to do better. I wouldn't choose to wake up at 6 am to take a walk for my health, but I did it for her. I made sure she ate even if there wasn't time to feed myself. She gave love without conditions, and I mirrored that. She also taught me about the importance of the quality of love that I was settling for. She rescued me from a bad pattern of giving myself and my time to men who were not great for me. After her arrival, I made better choices because that would be best for Peanut. She became my bridge to self-love.

Peanut had an innate ability to foster connections. She

greeted people with an open belly. Through her, I learned the power of vulnerability and authenticity, qualities that form the bedrock of genuine connections. She also taught me to ask (for a belly rub) to receive. She was a great judge of character and showered the people she loved with kisses. As I was raised in an emotionally conservative family, she taught me to be more demonstrative. In her view, kissing is acceptable anywhere. Her Yoda essence was telling me, "You must unlearn what you have learned. Try not. Do. Or do not." She taught me that all it takes to make friends is to walk around and say hi. Peanut made sure to greet all my clients when I was doing in-person sessions. During puppy socialization and obedience class, she was always at the top of her class, and she loved everyone. It was unusual when she showed her annoyance at an older husky puppy in her class who refused to train and would cry in complaint. It was as if she was telling the husky in a Yoda-like way, "Control, control, you must learn control."

Peanut's intuitive gifts were unparalleled. Her ability to sense energies and anticipate events transcended the mundane, offering glimpses into the mystical. My master spirit guide is over seven feet tall, and baby Peanut would often stare intently seven feet up and let out quiet woofs. She loved car rides and would place herself on my lap so that when I rolled down the car window, she would stick her head out, and her favorite was saying hello to drive-thru personnel. The unusual part was that no matter where our destination was, she would get excited about five minutes before we got there, even if I had never been there before.

Of course, she did normal dog things, but she also acted in extraordinary ways. Unlike many dogs who can only eat restrictive diets due to their sensitive digestion, she had a diverse diet that included vegetables and fruit. Also, Peanut knew when to stop eating. Other dogs would stuff themselves until they got sick. When I offered food when she was full, Peanut would turn her head in defiant refusal. As I was a stress eater, she was teaching me to be conscious about eating.

My mom was never fond of dogs and even had the gall to suggest I give Peanut away, but they bonded quickly, and my mom would often visit Peanut while I was at work. Every time my mom brought either a treat or toy for Peanut, she would store it and wouldn't touch it until I came home hours later and she could show me. As soon as I acknowledged her, she commenced eating or playing with zeal. That was never taught.

She loved balls and sticks but took things to the extreme. Since we lived near tennis courts, she loved finding tennis balls and bringing them home. At one point we collected two banker's boxes full of balls because I wasn't allowed to give or throw them away. And as far as sticks were concerned, the bigger the better. The park usually had good specimens, and each time she found a stick, she made sure to find progressively bigger sticks the next time. One day, she found a stick that was more than 4 1/2 feet long and she knew to pick it up from the center for balance and strutted home with her prize. She may have been too big to be a teacup, but her small size never stopped her. She embodied Yoda's quote, "Size matters not. Look at me. Judge me by my size, do you? Hmm? Hmm. And well you should not. For my ally is the Force, and a powerful ally it is. Life creates it, makes it grow. Its energy surrounds us and binds us. Luminous beings are we, not this crude matter."

I had the most magic-filled moments in the company of Peanut. Often, on our walks, hummingbirds and butterflies would accompany us. Hummingbirds would hover for extended periods or do flybys over her head. Once, on a walk, Peanut and I saw a butterfly in someone's garden. I felt the urge to hold out my finger, and immediately, the butterfly landed and stayed for a while. One day at dusk, while on another walk, we stopped at the stair landing because three green-blue lights at varying heights seemed to slowly meander and rise from below the stairwell toward the blue-violet ombre night sky. We both just watched until they disappeared. Los Angeles does not have fireflies. Nothing could explain what we saw. There have been a handful of times when bright white lights were floating around in my bedroom at night. I have blackout blinds, so it couldn't have been a reflection of any light source.

Peanut was also with me when I got the biggest sign from the universe to my nagging question of whether or not I should be healing full-time. I asked for a sign in the form of a hummingbird feather. It's not common to see. A few weeks later, I saw a tiny feather at the bottom of the stairwell of my apartment. I'm near-sighted so I couldn't believe I spotted this tiny feather. Since I couldn't fully believe it, I asked for another sign. Please show the hummingbird feather coming off a hummingbird's butt. A few weeks later, during my morning walk, a hummingbird flew over Peanut's head at my head level. It flew so close that I could feel the breeze from its wings. When I looked back to see where it came from, I found two hummingbird feathers floating gently down to the ground. Not sure if they were butt feathers, but I didn't risk another ask.

Sadly, Peanut's time with me was brief. She departed after a mere decade, leaving behind a legacy of love and wisdom. Her Force started diminishing when she was nine years old. Despite my taking her to multiple vets and specialists, no one was able to diagnose her with hepatic encephalopathy until it was too late. She was born with a smaller-than-normal liver size, and it should have presented when she was a puppy, but because I was a healer, the signs didn't show up until she was nine and was considered geriatric. Sadly, all of the vets didn't even consider congenital issues until it was too late. Towards the end, she started getting urinary tract infections, peeing inordinate amounts, and staring blankly into space.

Through Peanut's ordeal, I now know what illness and impending death look like. When my mom recently had a urinary tract infection after her pelvic fractures, she had that far-away look, and I knew I had to take swift action to get her hospitalized. Peanut saved my mom's life. I use what I learned from Peanut to help others.

When she was ready to leave me for the spirit world, Peanut gave me a goodbye sign. She put her favorite toys in her bed, including the first toy I ever bought her. She had never put toys in her bed before. Her passing was marked by divine synchronicity on 3/3/2020. The number 33 is a master number and a symbol of divine guidance. It is linked to balance, compassion, blessings, inspiration, discipline, courage, and building the life you want to live, which are all qualities that Peanut embodied and also wished for me. Numbers 2020 is a message of transformation, new beginnings, awakening, and spiritual growth.

In her physical absence, grief weighed heavily upon me, a testament to the depth of our bond. Yet even in death, Peanut's presence lingered, a source of solace and guidance. The day after she left the physical world, I started getting unsolicited daily emails from Daily Pnut. Their motto is "World in a Nutshell". I promised Peanut I would show her the world, and now she is returning the favor with her daily messages. After her passing, I began to hear "Memories" by Maroon 5, a beautiful song about remembering the loved ones we've lost. When I talk to her or ask her to send me a sign, she sends this song. Like the Force, she is still very much with me. As I continue on my spiritual path, I carry her wisdom in my heart, forever grateful for the magic she brought into my life.

Bio

YuSon Shin is a gifted healer, intuitive, medium, speaker, author of nine books, and teacher of the healing and intuitive arts based in Los Angeles. With her trademark joyful and compassionate demeanor, she uses her gifts to help people and pets heal from physical, emotional, and spiritual ailments. YuSon loves teaching and holds workshops designed to help students awaken their spiritual superpowers. She believes everyone has the power to heal themselves.

YuSon is an expert practitioner in a wide variety of healing techniques because she feels there is no "one size fits all" when working with her clients. She utilizes Akashic records and Chinese energy healing techniques to perform past life, karma, and ancestral clearings. She is also a practitioner of the Bengston Energy Healing Method. She is a certified Reiki Master and also uses Integrated Energy Therapy, 5th Dimensional Quantum Healing, Quantum Touch, DNA Theta, and Access Bars.

She can be reached at YuSon@ShinHealingArts.com and www.ShinHealingArts.com.

Chapter Eighteen
By the Grace of a Dog
By Alicia Sweezer

There have been many animals in my life that had a massive effect or completely transformed my life. It was hard to choose which animal to write about for this book. And as always, the universe guided me. This story is about my dog Boomer. How could it not be? He is the first of many animals that saved my life. This is a story that no one knows because it is a story I've never told, till now.

Boomer was a Norwegian Elkhound (think Husky, but more fur). I was 14 years old, and he was a Christmas gift for my dad and me. Honestly, the cutest puppy ever! We hadn't had a puppy in the family in a long time. It was amazing in the beginning, and as the normal puppy challenges arose, it became difficult. Puppies chew things, like everything! Boomer enjoyed eating our wooden kitchen table and chairs. This was somehow my fault, even though I was a kid. I did everything I could to dissuade him, and he just wasn't having it. I think this is where my love of strong-willed and mischievous animals began.

When he became old enough, I did all the training with him. I took him to class and walked him every day. I, of course, loved all of this. Well, maybe not so much in the winter; we were in Michigan, after all. There were a lot of challenges in my family during those years. People in my life struggled with addiction, mental illness, financial challenges and much more. As children in these situations often do, we automatically believe it is all our fault—that somehow, we are responsible for everything. If we got better grades or did our chores, then we would be safe, and our parents would be happy. To say that I was desperate for love and emotional safety would be an understatement. And I found the unconditional love I was searching for in the place that it always has been in my life, from animals.

I was always better with animals than people. And yes, I fully admit that being an animal communicator does help. As a psychic child, I didn't cope well with the challenges in my childhood. How could I? I wasn't taught any tools for this or anything else. And truthfully, no one in my family was taught life skills or coping tools, either. Everyone was doing the best they could with what they had. I attempted to adapt by trying to be perfect, people please, and be as invisible as possible. To manage the fear and pain, I could have easily been a kid who cut themselves or worse. And honestly, because I was a "good" kid, no one would have had any idea. Well, no person, that is. Boomer knew, Boomer always knew.

When things became more difficult at home, and I secretly became suicidal, I turned to Boomer. He was my balance, my love, my joy, and he was my tether to this world. I could never leave him behind, and so I stayed. I stayed, held on tight, navigated the waves, and started to fulfill my dreams and my purpose for this lifetime. Boomer listened to me every night when I shared my fears and my dreams. He knew I would make it through even when I didn't.

Back then, I didn't know that I was psychic or an empath. So, to say I had a conscious understanding of what Boomer was doing would be inaccurate. All I know and remember was the feelings. When I was with him, I felt different. Every night when we sat together and talked, I unconsciously allowed his energy to envelop and heal me; it kept me going. Every time he made me laugh with his favorite toy (a plastic milk jug, of all things), it changed me. Every time he gave me that sly smile, and I knew what he was going to do, he helped grow my gifts. Except for the one time he swallowed an alive wild bird in one gulp, I didn't expect that! He didn't like birds because they stole his food. I still don't know how he physically accomplished that, and it left a mark on me for sure. He also liked to steal my parents' cigarettes. Remember that bratty side I spoke about?

Through training him, this quiet 16-year-old learned a little confidence, which, trust me, was no small feat. The dog trainer named him the social butterfly of the class. Yes, this introvert had a super extroverted dog (remember when I said he was my balance). Being the social butterfly is also how he became chunky because all our neighbors loved him and gave him treats constantly (full-size treats!). Even after he was on a diet, they would still sneak treats to him. I told you he was cute, fluffy, and mischievous. He knew how to use those big brown eyes to get anything he wanted!

Boomer kept me going and healing me in his way for many years. He lived a long life and continued to give to everyone around him. I am able to tell this story today and change this world for the better by the grace of a dog.

Thank you to Boomer and all my other soul animals. I love you always.

I invite everyone reading this book to ask yourself these questions:

What has your animal taught you?

What can you still learn from them?

Where can you give to them and create an amazing relationship with them?

P.S. Humans think they are the most intelligent among all the species. I can tell you from a lifetime of experience with animals as a wildlife biologist and an animal communicator this is not true. In case you don't believe me, I invite you to try to make a bird's nest with only your mouth. My fellow humans, let's be enormously grateful for our opposable thumbs, as they are our saving grace!

Bio

Alicia Sweezer, a scientific psychic and former wildlife biologist specializing in endangered species, embodies resilience and authenticity. Her journey is a testament to defying conventional boundaries and embracing one's true calling. With a unique blend of analytical prowess and intuitive gifts, Alicia empowers clients to catalyze profound shifts in mindset, behavior, and relationships.

As an Animal Communicator and Medium, Alicia extends her transformative abilities to the non-human realm, fostering deep connections between animals and their human counterparts. Her life story is marked by triumph over adversity, from overcoming career skepticism to healing after multiple traumatic brain injuries. Alicia's unwavering determination and courage inspire others to break free from limiting beliefs and embrace their innate potential.

Alicia Sweezer is not just a survivor; she is a beacon of hope, reminding us that anything is possible when we dare to embrace our truth. Alicia's passion for guiding others towards fulfillment and purpose resonates through her best-selling books, where she shares wisdom gleaned from her own journey of self-discovery and empowerment. With a message of boundless possibility, Alicia Sweezer invites all to connect with their truth and unleash their unique gifts upon the world. Connect with Alicia at: www.whoknewhealing.com

"It is a joy and privilege for me to serve our pets. The world would never be the same without these rays of light, love, wisdom, and joy."

Kristen West

Chapter Nineteen
Animal Teachers
By Kristen West

I have the best job in the world! As a small animal veterinarian, I have devoted most of my life to the care and service of animals. I am so grateful to be able to help God's creatures and their human families. No two days are the same in my job, and I have been able to treat scaled, feathered, furry, and not-so-furry pets. I have also been able to help with some wildlife care over the years.

In my amazing career and with my own pets throughout my life, I have had so many deeply personal, meaningful, life-changing encounters with animals. It is impossible for me to come up with just one story to tell in this chapter. Therefore, I have decided to focus on some lessons that I have learned from caring for animals.

1. Unconditional love exists.

There is a very special bond between people and their animal companions. Our pets love us no matter how we look, what mood we're in, what we do or don't say. Animals have no ulterior motive in giving love or receiving love. People could learn so much from animals in this respect.

My most personal experiences of unconditional love have come from my own pets. I have always had cats, and they have each been a daily source of joy and comfort. In times of grief, loss, and stress, I have always had a steadfast companion. Where people sometimes have failed me, my pets never have.

Professionally, I have had the honor to witness this loving relationship between my patients and their families. When people come in with their new pets, their faces glow with joy and pride. Animals light up the worlds of those who choose to adopt them. They inspire people to leave their comfort zones, learn to care for dependent creatures, and find extreme joy in doing so. It is a pleasure to witness pets at all stages of life and the relationships they forge with their families.

Our pets enrich our lives and can give people a reason to live.

2. Every day is full of learning opportunities.

Veterinary medicine, as with many professions, is dynamic and ever-changing. As science evolves, so does our understanding of the creatures we treat. I'm 24 years out of veterinary school, and I still run across conditions that are new to me or find myself researching new treatments for different ailments.

I love to watch animals learn. Seeing the unbridled joy of a young animal as they experience the world for the first time never gets old. I am often fascinated by the tricks and behaviors that animals can learn and master. Service dogs and therapy pets are miracles to those they help. As pet owners, we usually find that our pets train us as much as we train them!

Most people will tell me that their pets teach them something every day. Our capacity to learn about these animals, to make their domestic lives as fulfilling and stimulating as possible, and to strive for the best health and longevity for these beloved family members only grows as we learn more and more about them.

I feel that we will never stop learning from and being educated on behalf of these animals that we love.

3. Earned trust is a special gift.

Another life lesson that I learn from animals is trust. I am constantly amazed that most pets that we treat are accepting of the exams and sometimes painful procedures that we have to do to help them.

When I think about how I would feel if I was taken to an unknown building, restrained by a giant, manipulated, poked with needles, and sometimes anesthetized without any understanding of why, I can only imagine feeling terror!

However, most pets that we see are very tolerant, sometimes even happily greeting us with rumbling purrs and wagging tails. We do our best to put them at ease with treats and cuddles, but the vet office is probably still intimidating.

Trust is never more apparent than when an injured animal submits to treatment, even when painful. They often seem to understand that we are helping them.

We work with rescue groups and often see animals who have been badly mistreated and some who have never experienced kindness from people. We see many dogs who have lived in horrendous puppy mill situations, some who have never been allowed to be on grass or even to leave their small cages. We have the benefit of seeing these pets paired with patient foster families and safe new homes. We get to watch them come out of their shells and learn to trust again. Those who volunteer with these animals are among my heroes.

Earned trust from another creature is a sacred gift. I will never take this lightly.

4. It is okay to let go.

Admittedly, one of the most difficult and heart-wrenching aspects of my job is to euthanize pets. Many people say to me, somewhat insensitively, that they could never do what I do because they love animals too much. I would maintain that my love for animals is so great that I am willing to break my own heart to prevent undue suffering for them.

To believe euthanasia is a kindness is the only way that I can go forward. To have the honor of witnessing an animal's passing can be equally heartbreaking and spiritual. I can be there for the families, and I can share in their grief and try to help them. Together, we help to facilitate a soul's transition in a peaceful, loving manner.

I have witnessed so many unbelievable moments of love and acceptance in these instances. Pets often seem to tell their families when it's time. I have seen last loving gestures from animals to their people in their last moments, as if to comfort those who have cared for them the most. I have witnessed final hugs, kisses, and nudges. Animals seem to accept their transitions with peace and dignity.

In their short lives, animals leave such permanent marks on our hearts and lives.

To love, learn, trust, and let go are only some of the amazing lessons that I have been taught in my dealings with animals. These creatures are among God's greatest gifts in this world. In my own life, animals are central to my happiness, fulfillment, stress control, and joy. I made a vow to spend my life in service of animals, and it is the easiest vow to keep. I plan to spend the rest of my life caring for, learning from, admiring, and loving the animals of this world, especially those we have adopted into our families. It is a joy and privilege for me to serve our pets. The world would never be the same without these rays of light, love, wisdom, and joy.

Bio

I am a happily married mom of two busy teenagers. When not at work, I can generally be found with my nose in a book and two very needy cats in my lap. I am a practicing veterinarian and adore my job, but I have always yearned to write. I decided that it is never too late to follow my dream, and I am thrilled to be contributing to this book.

kwestdvm@aol.com

Chapter Twenty

Whispers of Wisdom: A Journey through Animal Insights and Personal Discoveries

By Hellevi Woodman

As I stood in the Ana Kai Tangata cave on the remote island of Rapa Nui in Chile (also known as Easter Island), I was immediately struck by the ancient petroglyphs etched into the walls. There, in all its glory, was the manutara, a sacred bird central to the island's Birdman cult. Standing in the hallowed cave, it struck me that the manutara and the other animals featured in the etchings were considered so sacred that they were immortalized on these walls. I thought back to the time when humans and animals were connected and spoke a common language, a time when man looked to animals for wisdom and learning.

Three thousand miles away, high in the Andes mountains of South America, I listened to the Q'ero shaman's elders as they spoke of their four sacred allies: the serpent, jaguar, hummingbird, and condor. They carefully explained how each animal represents a different aspect of healing and wisdom: the serpent's knowledge, the jaguar's courage, the hummingbird's appreciation for joy, and the condor's broad perspective.

The elder's teachings helped me see that animals were not just part of my life story; rather, they were integral to the tapestry of my being. Animals have taught me about the world, myself, and the boundless capacity of the heart. I knew I could see the world anew by embracing the wisdom of animals.

As a first step, I allowed the wisdom of the four allies to guide me in my own life. Embracing the serpent's wisdom, I began to let go of beliefs that no longer served me, engaging in the regular practice of self-reflection and meditation. The jaguar's courage guided me to confront fears I had previously let cripple me, allowing me to take bold steps toward my goals and tackle challenges head-on. The hummingbird taught me to actively seek out the nectar of life, maintaining a gratitude journal to remind me of life's small yet significant joys. And finally, by embodying the condor's perspective, I began to practice mindfulness and to view situations from a broader perspective.

Animals in Our Dreams

After embracing the wisdom of the four allies in my waking life, I found that the journey with animals extended into the realm of dreams, where they continued to serve as guides and teachers.

In my own life, dreams featuring animals have often felt like echoes of a deeper, more ancient wisdom, threading through my tapestry of experiences with animals both in waking life and in the realm of sleep. Once, a vivid dream of a majestic stag, bathed in moonlight, guided me through a dense forest, its antlers casting shadows that seemed to weave messages of resilience and grace under pressure. This dream came to me when I was navigating personal challenges, offering comfort and a sense of direction that felt eerily relevant.

In another instance, after a day spent volunteering at the animal rescue, I dreamed of a gentle but persistent turtle, reminding me, much like the creatures I had cared for, of the importance of patience and persistence. These dreams, coupled with my daily interactions with animals, suggest a personal and intimate language of symbols and signs that has guided me towards growth and understanding.

The animals I've encountered in my dreams, like those in

my waking life, have been teachers, friends, and guides, reflecting my innermost fears, hopes, and aspirations. They are not mere figments of the imagination but integral parts of my journey, offering insights and lessons that resonate with the wisdom shared by cultures and traditions around the globe.

This personal connection to animals in dreams underscores a universal truth: that we are all connected in the web of life, with animals as our companions and guides, speaking to us in the language of dreams, a language that transcends the barriers of the conscious mind to touch the soul.

Animals and History

Animal wisdom is ingrained in the fabric of human history and, in many ways, can serve as a guide on a path of self-discovery. Animals remind us of our deep connection to the natural world and our inner nature.

The Chinese zodiac and Mayan astrology, both rich in cultural heritage, use animals to offer insights into human nature and spirituality. From the Chinese zodiac's dragon to the jaguar featured in Mayan astrology, a universal theme emerges that animals guide and enrich our understanding of life's cycles and our place within them.

Yoga is another ancient practice that embraces the animal form with poses such as downward facing dog and the cobra pose, connecting us physically to animal qualities such as strength, agility, and grace.

For centuries, animals have been revered for their wisdom and strength. In Egypt, for example, cats were revered as symbols of grace, protection, and mysticism. In ancient Egyptian mythology, the goddess Bastet, often depicted as a lioness or as a woman with the head of a cat, was worshipped for her protective qualities. Cats, in Egyptian culture, were seen as guardians of the underworld, as well as protectors. They symbolized the ability to see the unseen and to navigate the mysteries of life and death, reflecting the importance of intuition in our lives.

The Hindu traditions have a deep respect for animals and the lessons they teach us. There are several Hindu deities that animals represent. Hanuman, for example, is a monkey god who embodies strength, valor, and devotion. Ganesha, who has an elephant head, is revered as the god of beginnings and the remover of obstacles. He symbolizes wisdom, understanding, and a discriminating intellect. Shiva, another Hindu god, is often depicted with a serpent around his neck, representing the power of creation and destruction. In yoga and spiritual practices, the serpent also represents kundalini energy, which is a source of primal energy and spiritual enlightenment. The cow is also considered sacred in Hinduism. It symbolizes abundance and non-violence and is revered for its gentle nature and for providing nourishment without expecting anything in return.

In Tanzania, the lion represents strength and leadership and is highly respected by the Maasai tribes. These tribes have a profound knowledge and admiration for wildlife, and their way of life is influenced by animal behavior, which reflects sustainable cohabitation practices. This long-standing relationship between humans and animals is best exemplified in the Serengeti and Ngorongoro regions, where it symbolizes a centuries-old symbiotic relationship.

The Kumulipo is a traditional Hawaiian creation chant that tells the story of how life emerged from the depths of the ocean. This chant connects the origins of humans with the animal kingdom, with ancestral spirits taking the form of creatures such as sea turtles and sharks. These animals are revered as family protectors and guides and help to create a harmonious bond between the natural and spiritual worlds.

According to the legends of the Māori people of New Zealand, the kiwi sacrificed its ability to fly to protect the forest, choosing a life of darkness on the ground to save the trees. The kiwi demonstrates selflessness for the greater good, a commitment to a cause greater than itself.

In Australia, the Aboriginal culture incorporates dreamtime stories that revolve around animals. Among these animals, the kangaroo is often featured as a symbol of resilience, capable of enduring long journeys across harsh terrains. Similarly, in Native American cultures, certain animals, such as the wolf, are considered spiritual guides or totems, symbolizing connections and emphasizing the importance of community.

A story from the Lakota tribe speaks of a lone wolf who, by trusting his intuition, led his pack to safety during a harsh winter, illustrating the value of trusting one's inner voice. Similarly, the Celtic traditions of Europe view the stag as a symbol of wisdom that serves as a messenger between the worlds.

During my visit to Oaxaca, Mexico, I had the opportunity to witness the Day of the Dead celebrations. It was a fascinating experience for me, as I got to observe various animals that hold spiritual significance to the locals. For instance, I was amazed by the monarch butterfly, which is believed to embody the spirits of the deceased and represent the cyclical nature of life. Similarly, the Xoloitzcuintli dog is considered to be a spiritual guide in the afterlife. Lastly, the brightly colored alebrijes caught my attention with their fantastical appearance.

Animals in Our Lives

While it is true that stags, wolves, and Hindu gods are exotic and mysterious, we gain so much joy and wisdom from the animals who join us in our everyday lives. Pets are so much more than just companions; they can be guides and teachers, mirrors reflecting the complexity of human emotions and resilience. From my earliest memories, the animals in my life played a significant role, offering lessons in love, loss, and the art of living.

As a child, I learned of unconditional love and companionship from my little grey kitten, a gentle presence whose soft purring was a soothing balm during times of family disharmony. To think that a tiny kitten provided me with stability amidst the chaos is quite remarkable.

My pet dog, an old and wise beagle, was my solace amidst the tumultuous sea of adolescence. He offered comfort and a sense of security, grieving with me in silence when I lost my father; his presence was a language, speaking directly to my heart.

This experience opened me to the importance of presence and non-verbal communication. Animals communicate in intricate, multilayered ways that include body language and energy perception. My interactions with animals helped me reflect on the depth and breadth of my human interactions. I learned to use body language and my energy to communicate more effectively with others. I became more aware of my non-verbal cues, and I strove to understand others beyond just words.

My pets have shown me that animals teach us so much about the giving and receiving of love and care. Becoming a mother gave me a new appreciation for my childhood cats who minded their kittens with the perfect balance of care and discipline. When my daughter grew into a mischievous toddler, watching my dog playfully interact with her—even when she became far too boisterous—was a masterclass in patience.

Fostering over 50 rescue dogs and volunteering at a rescue center taught me about resilience. Animals show remarkable adaptability, adjusting to new environments and situations easily. I marveled as I watched them fall into place within their complex societies, which were hierarchical, yet each member played a unique and essential role, mirroring our human communities. Their resilience in adapting to these ever-changing environments is a testament to their strength and versatility. Observing their resilience reminded me to be more flexible and open to change, accepting life's curveballs with grace and positivity.

My work with rescue dogs also opened my eyes to the challenges of loving without attachment and the harsh reality that sometimes love is not enough. I still remember the profound sadness of realizing that the handsome young pup I was caring for had trauma so deep that no amount of love could heal. These experiences were lessons in letting go and accepting the natural cycle of life and death, which made me a better caregiver and deepened my understanding of compassion and empathy.

Embracing the Fun

Animals provide ample opportunities for deep thought and introspection, but let's not forget that they're also loads of fun! My pet beagle had a knack for making my baby sister laugh so hard that it often led to an entire room being engulfed in laughter. Our chickens gave me and my brother the opportunity to engage in hilarious egg hunts, and our parrots were well known for their mischievous antics, which I confess led to equal parts amusement and frustration. (Realizing my parrot had made a mess of my school uniform seconds before running out the door indeed taught me to embrace life's unpredictable moments.)

The joy that comes from being present is yet another skill I learned from watching my pets engage and interact with others. Whether it's a dog chasing a ball, a cat basking in the sun, or a parrot showing off his latest trick, animals are completely absorbed in the now, undistracted by past regrets or future anxieties. By incorporating this level of mindfulness into the simple activities in my own life, I have found more joy and gratitude.

Reflecting on My Animal Journey

When I reflect deeply on the countless ways in which animals have enriched my life, I am overwhelmed with gratitude. Their behaviors, their non-verbal communication, and their adaptability have imparted me with a wealth of wisdom. Animals have been my guides, teaching me about the beauty of our world and the depth of our human spirit. Their teachings are universal, timeless, and profoundly impactful.

My journey with animals has been transformative, inspiring me to bring awareness to the value of all life forms and to live more consciously, considering my impact on this planet and the legacy I wish to leave behind.

So, as I sit here surrounded by my three loving rescue dogs, I contemplate the mutual connection we humans share with animals—a bond that educates, heals, and enhances our lives. And I think to myself, how truly lucky we are.

Dedication

To all the amazing animals around the world, thank you. This chapter is my humble tribute to honor the special bond between humans and animals, a bond that has lasted throughout history and across this planet. It celebrates how animals have been our teachers, friends, and helpers. I'm sharing stories from different cultures about animal wisdom and my own experiences with animals, each a testament to the profound and often unspoken language that unites all living beings. May this chapter show the beautiful connection we all share with our fellow earthlings and remind us of the deep wisdom that resides in the heart of nature.

Bio

My name is Hellevi E. Woodman, and I am a Venezuelan American entertainer with over thirty years of experience in the arts. In 2012, I shifted my focus towards yoga, meditation, and holistic healing, and became a health coach, yoga instructor, Reiki practitioner, and ceremonialist. My passion lies in ancient wisdom, shamanic practices, breathwork, and sound healing, which have guided me throughout my journey. As an author and storyteller, I love to travel and explore the magical places on Earth, seeking out sacred tools for conscious living, dreaming, and dying. My journey is not just about personal growth but also about creating harmony, connecting with the universal energy that surrounds us, and tapping into the healing powers of nature.

hellevie@hotmail.com

"The pets and animals we invite into our lives are more than companions. They heal and guide us by reminding us of the best of who we are. Their support is unwavering. Their requirements are so simple and true. Mia and Lily's presence in my life at that exact time was no mistake. It was a gift from the universe to help me heal my deepest wounds."

Janet Zavala

Chapter Twenty-One
The Journey Home, Healing, and Self-Love
By Janet Zavala

In the tapestry of life, there are threads of sorrow, healing, and joy. These are the threads that bind us together in the most unexpected ways. For me, those threads were woven with the love and companionship of my beloved dogs, Mia and Lily. They taught me the true meaning of healing and creating a safe home while guiding me through some of my darkest days with unwavering love and devotion.

The cruelest reality of life reveals itself in the fleeting moments we share with our pets. Their lives, so vibrant and full of love, seem to slip through our fingers far too quickly, leaving behind an ache that remains for a lifetime. This overwhelming truth brought me to my knees on a somber day in January, as I bid farewell to my dear Mia. With tears streaming down my cheeks, I wrote down every cherished memory, every little detail that captured the essence of her spirit. Mia wasn't just a pet; she was family—a constant source of love and companionship.

My life, at times, has been a whirlwind of uncertainty and instability. Growing up, dogs were a part of my life, but they were never truly mine. In California, our dogs were safely housed, but in the more rural spaces of Illinois, where we later moved, they roamed freely, often not making it back home. When I ventured out on my own, I lived in rented apartments where pets were not allowed. The concept of permanence had always felt elusive. But with the purchase of my first house in May 2009, I finally found a place to call my own. This home wasn't just a house; it was my foundation—a grounding force that provided stability and security during one of my life's turbulent storms.

Sisters from the same litter, Mia and Lily, a mix of miniature pinscher and chihuahua, joined our family at eight weeks old. They brought much needed light and joy into our life from the moment they arrived. Mia, the smallest of the two, commanded the highest household rank. She had a regal demeanor, a distinctive bump on her nose, a pronounced underbite, and a habit of crossing her front legs like a lady. Her sister, Lily, bounced around full of youthful energy, matching my son's teenage vitality. Together, they formed the foundation of our family and marked our new beginning. They offered unwavering love and companionship during a time filled with uncertainty.

Together, they carved out a place in my heart that was uniquely theirs. The sisters shared a bond, often cuddling up next to one another. They also shared a competitive nature, as demonstrated on our walks in the neighborhood. They loved to walk single file on the narrow curb. If Lily happened to be in front of Mia, she would pass her and bump her off the curb so she could take her rightful place as the lead.

The pandemic brought with it an unexpected blessing—the gift of time spent in the company of my girls. No longer bound by the constraints of traveling to an office for my nine-to-five schedule, all three of us reveled in the constant companionship. Mia seemed to age at double the speed of Lily. Her face grew more and more gray hairs with each passing day, and her once vibrant spirit began to fade. Her playful indignance began to resemble more of a grumpy old lady.

As the years passed, I couldn't shake the inevitable truth looming on the horizon. Mia's health began to decline, and her boundless energy gave way to the ravages of age. On November 30th, 2022, at exactly 5:30 pm, Mia had her first seizure. It happens all the time with dogs, they said. I optimistically did all the things medically available to her. Two more seizures later, the cognitive decline was swift and painful to watch. I was internally negotiating extending her life. When her dementia escalated and she started circling the kitchen island for what seemed like hours (endless pacing is an advanced symptom of cognitive decline) and she couldn't stand to be gently touched, I knew that my desire for her to stay with me was selfish and causing more suffering.

In her final moments, Mia lay peacefully, her front legs crossed in a gesture of quiet dignity. It was a fitting farewell for the queen that she was—a reminder of the strength and grace that defined her spirit.

In the wake of Mia's passing, grief threatened to consume me. My heart was ripped in two. The pain was raw and unrelenting, a constant reminder of the void left by her absence. I had never felt this level of grief. These sisters have spent their entire lives with me—from puppy to old ladies. I held tightly to my son's message, "She lived a lavish life with you, Mom," for comfort.

But amidst the sorrow, there existed thirteen years of memories—a reminder of the love, healing, and joy Mia had brought into my life. And as I held onto Lily, knowing that time would continue to be the enemy, I found solace and gratitude that we still had each other. Sweet Lily, with her loving demeanor and gentle spirit, continues to grace my life with her presence.

As I navigate the twists and turns of my life, the sisters' place in this pivotal time in my life is cemented in my mind. Their presence, along with the stability of my new home, offered me a sense of security and grounding during a time of profound change, including a divorce, an empty nest, and an unwelcome career change. These significant life changes left me breathless. I am forever thankful for the healing power of my girls and the profound impact they have had on my life. They were my constant companions during the time when my life broke apart. They were forever by my side, witnessed every tear I cried, and joined me in bed every time I couldn't bring myself to get out of it. They were the silent observers when the light started to reemerge, and I began to rebuild my self-image and find my self-worth. They were there as I found strength and stability, always steadfast by my side, providing me with love when I felt my most unlovable.

The pets and animals we invite into our lives are more than companions. They heal and guide us by reminding us of the best of who we are. Their support is unwavering. Their requirements are so simple and true. Mia and Lily's presence in my life at that exact time was no mistake. It was a gift from the universe to help me heal my deepest wounds.

Consider your own experiences with animals and the ways in which they have touched your heart. Whether it's a playful puppy or a loyal companion, animals have a unique ability to offer comfort, companionship, and healing in our lives. The connection we make with them is on the deepest soul level. If we allow ourselves, we can be transformed by an animal's presence in our lives, no matter the length of time they spend with us.

Bio

Janet Zavala is a certified life and career coach, workshop creator and facilitator. She is a 5-time best-selling author of *The Nature of Transformation* and four compilation books. She is passionate about empowering women to navigate life and career transitions, discover their true potential, and create a life they love. Visit JanetZavalaCoaching.com to contact Janet and learn more about her services.

Animal Gallery

Baby Fritz

Willow Rose

Angel and Peace

Avery, Animal Protector

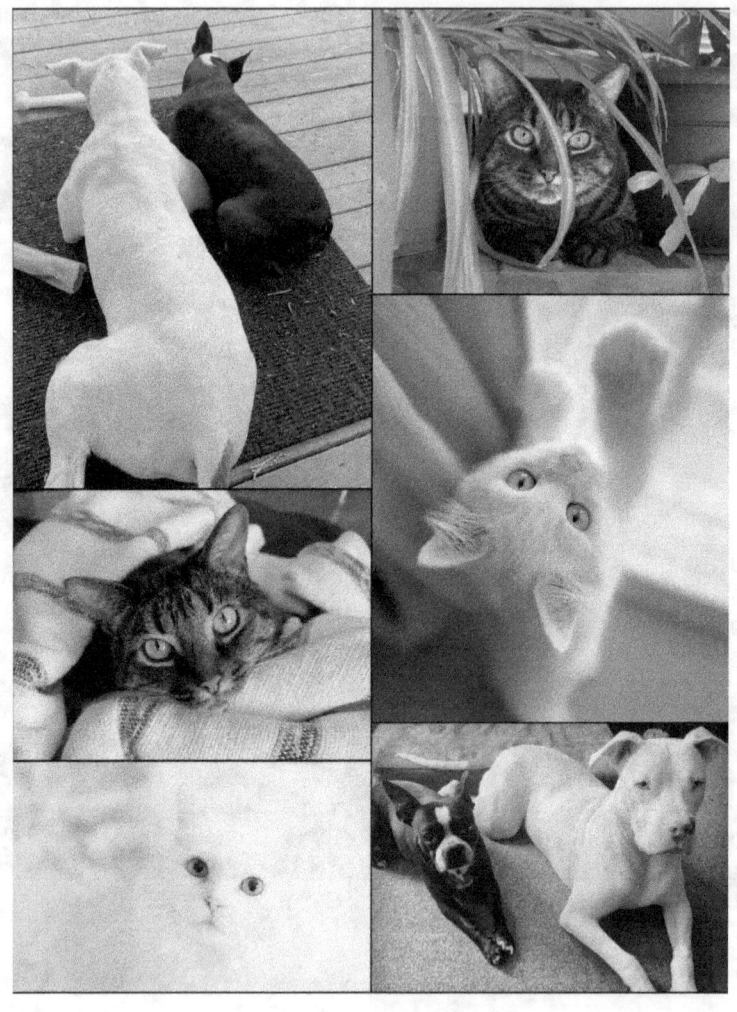

Princess

Patience

Pia, Sadie & Rocky

Boomer

Nevele

Peanut

Mia and Lily

Toutsie

Jack and Honey

Featured Authors

Amy I King

Amy I King is a Certified Life Coach, credentialed teacher, and the author of the best-selling book

Messy Wheels: Stories from Where I Sit. She is also a contributing author of fifteen international bestsellers, including *Inspirations: 101 Uplifting Stories for Daily Happiness, Manifestations: True Stories of Bringing the Imagined into Reality, The Grateful Soul: The Art and Practice of Gratitude, The Courageous Heart: Finding Strength in Difficult Times,* and *Ordinary Oneness: The Simplicity of Everyday Love, Grace and Hope,* and *365 Days of Self Love.*

When not writing, she enjoys music, movies, concerts, travel, exercising, practicing mindfulness through meditation, sunshine, reading, brunches and cardio drumming with her heart tribe.

Amy has overcome a plethora of challenges, including Spina bifida, narcissistic abuse, a personal cancer journey, and the losses of many loved ones from which she draws wisdom to assist clients.

Amy's greatest joy is using her personal experiences to help others move past their personal blocks and outdated beliefs to become empowered to live the life of their dreams. She is currently developing a program to help youth overcome trauma through their writing.

Her relationships with clients are built on trust and vulnerability. She welcomes the opportunity to work with you to help you transform your life into the phenomenal one that you deserve!

Contact @ Amy.kinglifecoaching@gmail.com

Beth Eiglarsh

Beth is a Neurolinguistics Programming Life Coach, Advanced Practitioner Reiki Master in Usui, Kundalini & Lightarian modalities, Holographic Memory Resolution Trauma-informed Healer, Spiritual Teacher, and Empathic Intuitive. She is a perpetual student, continually expanding her knowledge to better serve those around her. As a "master perspective shifter," her greatest passion comes from empowering others to see the world, themselves, and their story in a more positive light. Beth's understanding of the soul's divine purpose fuels her mission to support others in turning their unique journey into a springboard for living their most fulfilling lives.

Beth's spiritual awakening was prompted by her struggle with chaos, chronic pain, and workaholism. After an intense introspective process, followed by a radical pivot, she developed a system for living to help others navigate their lives with greater ease and grace. Beth teaches her 4-step A.R.M.S formula to groups and individuals who are looking to raise their level of *Awareness*, *Remember* who they are, *Manifest* their desires, and be of *Service* to themselves and others.

An "International Best-Selling Author", Beth penned *Beth's Case Scenario; Journey From Chaos To Emotional Freedom*, now available in audiobook format. Paws and Purpose is her 5th collaborative book with As You Wish Publishing, Inc., and she is immeasurably grateful for the connections made. Beth values the wisdom she acquired through her transformational experience and seizes every opportunity to help people feel better by offering one-on-one sessions, workshops, and Mind, Body, and Spirit retreats. For more information, go to www.SpeakToBeth.com

Janet Zavala

Janet Zavala is a certified coach, workshop facilitator, and bestselling author with over 35 years of experience in the corporate environment, including 15 years dedicated to coaching individuals and groups. She is an accomplished leader and career coach, guiding numerous staff members and clients to achieve their career aspirations.

Her expertise extends to creating dynamic personal

and professional workshops, which she has delivered to hundreds of attendees both virtually and in-person. Janet has crafted original training materials, workbooks, and journals designed to enhance participant learning during and after these transformative sessions.

As a five-time bestselling author, Janet's first solo book, "The Nature of Transformation," along with four compilation books, has captivated readers and received critical acclaim.

Janet Zavala is driven by a deep passion for empowering professional women and those in midlife to unlock their true potential, embark on transformative journeys in their lives and careers, and forge paths that resonate with joy and fulfillment. Her expertise lies in assisting individuals in cultivating confidence, shedding limiting beliefs that hinder their progress, and embracing their innate strengths to reach new heights of success. Janet's support extends to guiding her clients in crafting authentic, balanced, and fulfilling lives that align with their aspirations and values.

She combines her experience using proven coaching methods, results-oriented business strategies, and her own experience navigating personal and professional reinventions to guide her clients to create their own powerful transformations.

Discover Janet at:

Website: JanetZavalaCoaching.com

Email: Janet@JanetZavalaCoaching.com

Follow Janet Zavala Coaching on social media

Karen Gabler

Karen Gabler is an award-winning attorney, intuitive mentor, psychic medium, animal communicator and Reiki master. She is also a teacher, inspirational speaker, and internationally best-selling author. Karen is passionate about encouraging others to find their highest purpose and live their best lives, while overcoming life challenges and past traumas. She mentors her clients through a variety of personal and business issues, marrying her practical legal and business experience with her innate intuitive ability to receive information and guidance from higher sources. She also facilitates connections with clients' loved ones in spirit and offers life guidance obtained through her spiritual connections. Karen conducts workshops and presentations on a variety of business, spiritual and personal development topics.

Karen earned her Bachelor of Arts in psychology from the University of Hawaii and her Juris Doctorate from the William S. Richardson School of Law at the University of Hawaii. Karen has pursued wide-ranging education in interpersonal development and the spiritual sciences, working with multiple tutors from the prestigious Arthur Findlay College for the Psychic Sciences in England as well as with numerous intuitives and mediums throughout the United States. She has been a WCIT in the Martha Beck Wayfinder life coaching program. Her written work on spiritual and personal development topics has been published in thirteen collections of short stories published by As You Wish Publishing. Karen enjoys reading, hiking, horseback riding and spending time with her husband and two children. You can find Karen at www.karengabler.com.

Kristen West

I am a happily married mom of two busy teenagers. I grew up in Ohio and still live here. My husband and I share a love of books and reading and are desperately trying to pass this love down to our kids. When not at work, I can generally be found with my nose in a book and two very needy cats in my lap. I am a practicing veterinarian. Every day I get the privilege of taking care of peoples' pets. I adore my job, but I have always yearned to write. Submitting an entry like this is scarier than a dozen graduate school tests! I decided that it is never too late to follow my dream, and I am thrilled to be contributing to this book. kwestdvm@aol.com

Kyra Schaefer

Kyra Schaefer, Co-Founder and CEO of As You Wish Publishing, a venture established with her husband, Todd Schaefer, has dedicated the past seven years to empowering individuals to illuminate their unique essence and share their narratives with the world. Leading As You Wish Publishing, Kyra spearheads the publication of collaborative and solo books, available in print and ebook formats.

The diverse array of books produced by As You Wish Publishing, whether authored individually or through collaboration, cover a broad spectrum of topics such as self-discovery, personal journeys, healing, holistic business, therapeutic modalities, coaching, and spirituality. Kyra, alongside her husband, has successfully collaborated with numerous authors, embracing a variety of ages, writing styles, and creative approaches.

Beyond her role as a bestselling and award-winning author renowned for "Holograms and Echoes: Transform Triggers to Truth," Kyra Schaefer's passion extends to creating empowering, joyful, and insightful workshops tailored for small groups. Her expertise also spans certifications in Positive Psychology, Art Therapy, and as a Master Practitioner in Neurolinguistics and Hypnosis. With a rich career spanning two decades, Kyra has positively impacted thousands of clients in her role as an emotional therapy practitioner.

Reach Kyra at connect@asyouwishpublishing.com or via the web at www.asyouwishpublishing.com

Rosanne Groover Norris

Rosanne Norris embarked on a spiritual path in 2018 after her thirty-year-old son, Lee, passed unexpectedly. She is an affiliate leader and caring listener for Helping Parents Heal, an organization to help parents, after the loss of a child.

Rosanne is an author of beLEEve, a Journey of Loss, Healing, and Hope (2020), and a contributor to three anthologies: Ordinary Oneness, The Simplicity of Everyday Love, Grace and Hope (2021), Gathering at the Doorway, An Anthology of Signs, Visits, and Messages from the Afterlife (2022), and Ignite Your Inner Fire (2023). Rosanne was also featured in the award-winning documentary, "Rinaldi," the story of Brazilian trans-communication researcher, Sonia Rinaldi, who for over thirty years has brought through images and voices from deceased loved ones.

Additionally, Rosanne is a Reiki Master and a certified grief educator, trained by the world-renowned David Kessler.

She can be reached at rmnorris457@gmail.com

Dr. Sally Nazari

Dr. Sally Nazari is a licensed psychologist offering an integrative psychospiritual practice in the USA. Following her attainment of a doctoral degree in clinical psychology with distinction, she went on to train as a spiritual practitioner before becoming a Certified Spiritual Advisor. Dr. Nazari completed training in somatic modalities, a 500-hour Registered Yoga Teacher and a 200-hour Certified Meditation Instructor, to complete the triad of expertise in mind-body-spirit modalities. Dr. Nazari is passionate about sharing psychological resources. She focuses on integrating empirically supported treatment and holistic approaches, which she has done in various settings throughout the USA. She has also been invited to author multiple publications in peer-reviewed journals and professional presentations and to hold leadership positions within international professional organizations.

Dr. Nazari has been a sought out featured speaker-trainer in such facilities as the New York Presbyterian Hospital, Helen Hayes Hospital, Good Samaritan Hospital, and law enforcement communities and school districts on a variety of topics. Dr. Nazari's distinctive approach and expertise have been sought out to consult on unique psychospiritual cases and settings. Additionally, she is a topic expert within the GoodTherapy.org community and has been featured in multiple media outlets. She has also authored several books, including an international bestseller and a book focusing on the emotional and relational aspects of social connectedness with companion animals. Dr. Nazari's passion for sharing psychological resources and tools also led to her dedication to hosting and broadcasting a podcast.

Website: www.drsallynazari.com
Email: drnazari@drsallynazari.com

Sarah Gabler

Sarah Gabler is 17 years old and a senior in high school. She adores spending time with her family and traveling to new places. Sarah loves riding her horse and playing ukulele, guitar, and keyboard. She is a lifelong artist and loves using creative outlets to express herself. Sarah is an internationally best-selling author and has been published in multiple collections of short stories with As You Wish Publishing. She works as a stage manager for musical productions and loves bringing shows to life to entertain others. Sarah plans to major in psychology and wants to study abroad during her college years. One of her proudest achievements is serving as the Co-Editor in Chief of her school's yearbook and turning it into the most diverse publication created in the school's history. Sarah believes in using creativity to facilitate strong mental health and plans to combine her interest in creative endeavors with her psychology studies to develop ways to make art and self-expression more accessible to all. Sarah began exploring self-development and soul empowerment concepts when she was just 10 years old and believes it has made her a better person today. It has motivated her to pursue her best life as well as to help others on their fulfillment journey. Sarah wants to empower people by helping them recognize their true potential. She believes that even the smallest acts of kindness can make someone's day, and she always tries her best to help others feel heard, seen and loved.

YuSon Shin

YuSon Shin is an international healer who has successfully helped both people and animals with physical issues like cancer, Covid-19, pneumonia, Lyme, high blood pressure, pancreatitis, kidney and digestive issues, and other diseases rooted in inflammation. As a highly trained intuitive and an animal lover, she enjoys using her skills as a medical intuitive and animal communicator to advocate for animals. In her experience, animals heal quickly because they don't have the high levels of baggage and complications that humans do. She believes everyone has the power to heal themselves, and as a healer, she simply accelerates healing by clearing the blockages, whether physical, emotional, generational/ancestral, past life, or trauma-based. YuSon also enjoys teaching humans to heal themselves and use their latent intuitive abilities. She also enjoys sharing her knowledge and empowering others through speaking engagements and her nine books.

She can be reached at YuSon@ShinHealingArts.com and www.ShinHealingArts.com.